THE MANCHESTER, BOLT(AND NAVIGATION COMPAI

In the latter part of the eighteenth century, the Duke of Bridgewater constructed a canal connecting his Worsley coal mines with Manchester. His efforts were doubly rewarded: the transporting of coal (which until then had had to be carried along the notoriously inadequate roads) became much more efficient, and the problems of colliery drainage were solved.

Matthew Fletcher, whose family were to become the biggest coal owners in the Irwell valley, quickly realised that the difficulties resolved by the Bridgewater Navigation were similar to those besetting himself and his associates in the Croal/Irwell valley. Spurred by the Bridgewater example, in 1790 he made a preliminary survey for a canal from Manchester to Bolton and to Bury.

Matthew was a far-sighted man and he lived in exciting times; a period in history when England was changing from a rural agricultural nation to the workshop of the world. He recognised the importance of the Croal/Irwell valley and the urgent necessity for an adequate and cheap form of transport for the goods being produced there.

Following the preliminary survey, an official survey was made in 1791 by Hugh Henshall, brother in law to James Brindley, the Duke of Bridgewater's consultant engineer. Parliament was petitioned in the same year and the Act of 1791 gave permission for the work to commence at once.

The canal was to be a total of 16 miles in length, with 17 locks and 3 aqueducts. The water supply (a very contentious matter in those times) was to be a reservoir constructed at Summerseat, augmented by drainage water from the local land and collieries. The estimated cost was £47,000, a figure which was revised and increased several times during the construction of the canal. The required capital was raised by the issue of shares, and the articles of association stipulated that no one person was to hold

****

Published in 1985 by Neil Richardson   *ISBN 0 907511 79 1*

Cover: Puddling gang near Nob End (Photo: D Stones). The publisher is indebted to the following for permission to use photographs and maps: Bolton Reference Library, Farnworth Library, Bolton Museum, Salford Local History Library, Swinton Library, Bolton Evening News, Mr D Stones, Mr J Santley, Mr F Sunderland.

more than £5,000 worth. The company was to be known as the Manchester, Bolton and Bury Canal and Navigation Company, and the principal shareholders were:

The Earl of Derby	£3,000
Sir J E Heathcote	£3,000
The Earl of Wilton	£2,000
Dr James Bent	£2,000

The remaining shares were held by the local industrialists and other public-spirited people.

The canal was to be cut from Church Wharf, Bolton, to Bury Wharf, with a flight of locks at Nob End joining a further canal to Oldfield Road, Salford.

Hardly had the first sods been lifted when thoughts were directed towards a link with the projected Leeds and Liverpool Canal at Red Moss near Wigan. Negotiations, albeit tentative ones, were put in hand. Work on the original canal went ahead at a spanking pace, and by 1793 progress had been made to the Prestolee Locks (Nob End). Until then, construction had been based on narrowboat traffic, but in view of the talks and the hoped-for amalgamation with the Leeds and Liverpool, it was decided that work would have to be revised to take vessels of barge proportions and dimensions. Lengths would have to be widened, bridgeholes enlarged and locks made bigger to take the longer and broader boats which the Leeds and Liverpool intended to operate. The locks had to be made to take two 68-foot narrowboats side by side or one 70-foot broadboat set askew.

To reorganise the work in hand and to restructure that already done meant another call on the shareholders; a further £20,000 over and above the original estimate was needed – almost half as much again. It was a very heavy call on the same pockets, but such was the faith in the future (or was it fear that if the call was not answered the Canal was doomed?) that the money needed was provided. In 1793 John Nightingale, nephew of the indefatigable Matthew Fletcher, was appointed Engineer to superintend the necessary alteration works – including those on the Bankside Aqueduct at Darcy Lever, a construction which in itself was an astonishing feat of canal engineering. The extra financial burden acted as an incentive and rapid progress was made; the first freight tolls from Oldfield Road to Rhodes Lock were taken in 1795.

Matthew Fletcher made certain that the Wet Earth Colliery drainage sough, built for him by Brindley in 1750, was connected to the main canal by a lock, giving him access to the Manchester market at an early date. Very soon the Fletcher interests at Clifton expanded and prospered; the sough was extended, a large, well-equipped boatbuilding yard with sawing facilities sprang up and an extensive area was used as a timber yard.

Trade on the new canal reached an unthought-of level of prosperity and still the idea of the Leeds and Liverpool connection was strong, so strong that land was purchased at Red Moss with the intention of making the connection at that point through a staircase of 30 locks. However, the Leeds and Liverpool people decided against the amalgamation because of "the mighty staircase of locks and their consequential heavy demand on the water supply." So for the time being the matter stood, but the idea was not abandoned by the Manchester, Bolton and Bury people and conversations to that end continued up to 1824, when the Leeds and Liverpool was connected with the Bridgewater Canal at Leigh.

The lure of Liverpool trade was constantly in the minds of canal companies; it was an attraction to those who used their facilities, as it would not only open up markets otherwise denied to manufacturers but also improve access to sources of raw materials - and at lower prices. The Manchester, Bolton and Bury Canal Company negotiated with the Manchester and Salford Junction Canal Company for the use of the Irwell Tunnel to obtain river connection, and by 1811 it was possible to travel from Bolton to Liverpool via the Mersey and Irwell Navigation.

The courtship between the Manchester, Bolton and Bury and the Leeds and Liverpool must have had many attractions, because despite the new through passage to Liverpool there were still people who wanted to join up with the Leeds and Liverpool Canal. It was next intended to connect the two waterways by a railway line running from Church Wharf to a point in Leigh. The railway was started but the two canals were never connected; the land at Red Moss was sold and the whole idea of amalgamation was put aside.

The very mention of the word "canal" conjures up the picture of a grimy, polluted waterway used by the local collieries as a cheap mode of transport. This may be true of the original idea; the building of the Manchester, Bolton and Bury Canal was vital to the progress and industrial expansion of the many under-takings in the Croal/Irwell valley, and the shipment of coal was the original motivation behind the building of the waterway. Yet very soon an extensive range of merchandise was being carried in addition to the coal: cargoes such as raw cotton, finished cotton goods, timber, bricks and stone for the hungry building industry, lime and manure, foodstuffs, milk, pottery, chemicals and salts - in fact, every conceivable kind of article was transported by canal. There was also a special parcel and package delivery service, but the speciality was the carriage of people by the passenger service.

By the late 1790's Manchester was the established market centre for the surrounding cotton towns and the Bridgewater Canal Company offered a frequent, well-organised passenger service to and from Manchester on the entire length of their navigation.

It was well patronised, not only by cotton merchants and manufacturers, but by everyone who had the call to travel to the town.

The Manchester, Bolton and Bury owners were quick to copy such enterprise and as early as 1796 (before the canal was completed) they anticipated a successful passenger service by building and launching their first passenger packet boat and appointing one James Parkinson to captain the vessel. Later in 1796 the first passengers embarked at Windsor Bridge for Bolton and journeyed along the unfinished canal.

The canal company had so much faith in the prospects of the passenger service that in 1797 the annual meeting of the Company passed the following minute:
"That a new boat of large construction for the purpose of a Packet shall be built by the Company, for its service, as soon as the money can be provided adequate to the expense."

The boat was built in 1798, the first of what was eventually to be a fair-sized fleet of such vessels plying the lengths of the Manchester, Bolton and Bury Canal. Many of these boats were named; the Agent's Journal of 1833 mentions that the *Fly* was damaged at Bury when a boat captained by a Thomas Dickenson ran into the stern. Dickenson was ordered to pay for the damage and duly got a bill for 11/8d. In another collision at Bolton the *Nelson* sprang a leak, and the year 1834 saw the new boat *Liverpool* in service.

The passenger service was held in such high esteem by the Company that its first bylaw gave preferential treatment to the carriage of passengers by ruling that: *"If any boat navigating the Canal do not drop its line and give way to the Packet Boat on the inner side in passing, the Manager of such a boat shall forfeit Ten Shillings."*

The service was from Church Wharf in Bolton to Oldfield Road in Salford, and from Church Wharf to Bury Wharf, with a service in the reverse direction. The first scheduled packets left Church Wharf and Oldfield Road on their respective journeys to Manchester and Bolton on 13th October 1795, when regular trips started. Throughout the whole period the service lasted, nearly 43 years, a very strict timetable was adhered to. Departure times, as laid down in the Company rules, were based on the times shown by the church clock in Bolton and the clock on St Ann's Church in Manchester.

The service grew in popularity, very soon becoming a specialised and highly profitable part of the canal transport undertaking, and there was quickly a call for passages to Bury. The passenger packet boats left at six o'clock in the morning and returned at five o'clock in the evening in the summer time. In winter departure was at seven o'clock in the morning, return at four o'clock in the afternoon. First Class cabin fares from

Bolton or Manchester in 1795 were 1/6d (single) and 2/6d (return). Second Class fares were 1/- (single) and 1/6d (return). The fares from Bolton to Bury and from Bury to Bolton were in proportion; in 1810 the fare for the eight mile journey was 2/- First Class return (1/4d Second Class return).

Patronage of the Bolton-Bury route was so good that it was possible to reduce the fares and in 1822 First Class return was 1/4d; Second Class return was 1/-. The fares were again reduced in 1830 (to 1/3d and 10d) and in 1832 there was a further reduction to 1/- and 9d respectively.

The traffic was in excess of 60,000 passengers per year; between July 1833 and June 1834 21,060 made the journey from Bolton to Manchester, 21,212 people travelled from Manchester to Bolton and 20,818 intermediary passengers hopped on and off the boats en route. Furthermore, during the month of May in that year, 1,324 sporting ladies and gentlemen travelled to Manchester Races. In the year 1834 the Bolton to Manchester service earned £1,177 and the Bolton to Bury service earned £75.

Travel in the late 1700's and early 1800's was not something lightly undertaken - in addition to the hazards and dangers to life and limb, it was most uncomfortable. When ordinary men and women travelled on foot and those without their own horses had to take a stage coach to journey any distance, it was only the most daring who ventured far outside their home parish boundaries of their own free will. That is, until the Manchester, Bolton and Bury Canal Company opened new horizons with their splendid passenger transport service.

A splendid service it was, as we note in the report of a young lady who made the journey from Bury to Bolton in 1825:

Our trunks were carried to the Boat by two maidservants, after a loud grand flourish on the horn and a loud 'Gee!' from the Captain we set off, two horses pulling on the ropes and we went on our way at three miles an hour.
The Boat was covered, having seats and tables inside, but if the weather was fine it was pleasant to sit outside in the forepart of the Boat.
A young woman in curlpapers and a coral necklace came to ask if anyone would take breakfast, which she would prepare in a little Cabin in the afterpart of the Boat, we never did have breakfast because it would have cost another shilling, but we did sometimes buy for tuppence currant cakes or peppermint drops which were brought round in a basket."

Canal passengers enjoyed unusually comfortable and generally safe travel for the most part, but in June 1818 a vessel going from Bury to Bolton suffered disaster. A party of drunken passengers brawling and fighting amongst themselves capsized the boat and several people, including two children, were drowned.

7

The first intention of the people who pioneered the waterway system was that it should carry merchandise and this it did very successfully for an exceptionally wide range of products. Such success made it necessary for an increasing number of people to travel in connection with their business interests and of course they found the passenger service very useful. Not only did it enhance the commercial and industrial interests in the region of its operations, but the social benefits of travel were of incalculable value. But it is important in these sophisticated times in which we live to consider that a journey from Bolton to Manchester was still a great adventure for the majority of the people. Those who regularly travelled between the two towns were looked upon as hardy souls. At the time this is being written (August 1983), there are certainly none of the people who made such a journey still alive, nor are there many detailed, personal, written accounts of such packet boat trips for the period 1795 to 1834. So we have to rely on verbal accounts handed on in the way canal lore has been, from one generation of canal people to the next, by the fireside in the home or at snap times in the boat dock cabins.

Can we undertake a trip along the Canal on a passenger Packet? The details of the journey will be correct, but we shall have to exercise a little imagination; never a bad practice, and very often a pleasantly rewarding one...

On the Bolton Canal, 1888

PART ONE

TAKE PASSAGE FROM BOLTON

The year is 1820, the day is a Tuesday in July, the time is five o'clock on a bright summer morning and people are about in the streets of Bolton. In twos and threes they all seem to be making for the same point – Church Wharf. There are men who from their appearance are men of business, there are clerics, handloom weavers looking for the best price for their products, chapmen with their cloth bundles, farmers and their wives with baskets of eggs and cheeses, some even struggling with cages of live poultry, others burdened with boxes of dressed fowl. All are bound for the distant town of Manchester, and all are intending passengers on the six o'clock passenger packet boat.

Stone steps lead down from street level to the cobbled wharf. There, in the shadow of the Parish Church, the Packet rides at moorings, smart with new paint, all brasses polished, the windows of the cabin reflecting the early morning sun. At the bow is a shining scythe blade which would sever the towing lines of any boat slow to give way. (Passenger packets have absolute right of way over all traffic – even over those boats engaged in the express delivery service.)

The Captain, resplendent in a braided frock coat, is busy seeing to the comfort of the passengers who have arrived early. Several dockhands are helping to stow the parcels and packages and on the towing path the ostlers are making adjustments to the harnesses of the two magnificent specimens of horseflesh which are the motive power of the Packet. The postilion, with cap and whip, looks on with obvious impatience. More and more passengers are now coming on to the wharf, then the last-minuters hurry aboard as the hands of the church clock creep nearer and nearer to 6.00am.

As soon as the hands of the clock show six and the mechanism begins to strike the hour, the Captain sounds the horn, the horseholders ease their animals into the collars, the postilion is astride the well-groomed, spirited lead horse, the hauling lines are taut and the dockhands push the boat into mid-channel with long barge poles. The water of the canal ripples back from the bows, the horses are at a walking pace and the journey has begun. The postilion looks back, satisfied that the boat is moving well, and he signals the horsehandlers to let go the bridles. Then, with loud shouting and much whipcracking, he increases the speed of the horses to a run and the Packet moves forward at a rapid rate.

Accommodation for the passengers is most comfortable. The cabin is divided into two sections – for'd for the First Class, who have paid 2/6d for the return journey, or 1/6d for the single

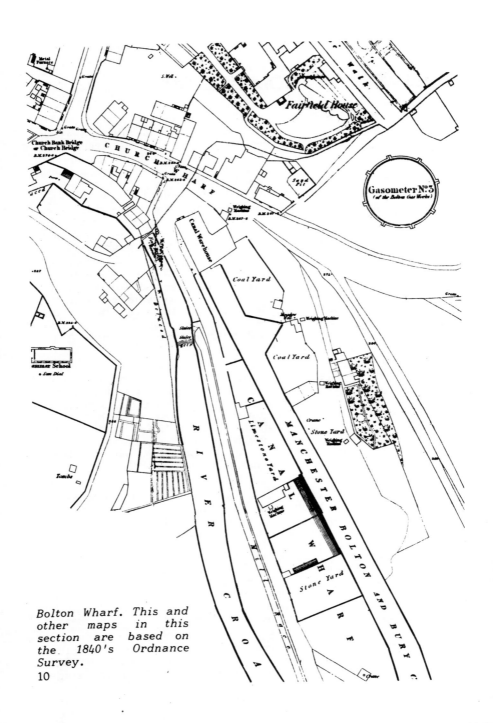

Bolton Wharf. This and
other maps in this
section are based on
the 1840's Ordnance
Survey.

10

trip to Manchester; seating is arranged down each side and down the centre are two tables, between which is a small iron stove set on an iron plate. There is a metal chimney up through the roof of the cabin to clear smoke and fumes when the stove is lit in winter. The after cabin for the Second Class is furnished on similar lines but on a plainer standard; the fare for this accommodation is 1/6d for the return or 1/- for the single trip. The cabins are clean and airy and the Company is proud of the fact that at the end of each trip the passenger accommodation is scrubbed and polished.

The peaceful silence of the cabin is suddenly shattered by the rattle of shod hooves over stone setts. The horn under the hand of the steersman Captain blares and the postilion is shouting fit to burst. The boat is coming up to a bridge and the horn and the shouting are warnings to any traffic on the far side that the Packet is approaching. Not by a single stride do the speeding horses falter; the postilion buries his face in the horse's mane and flattens his body along the animal's neck, the well-trained beasts swing on to the coping stones on the very edge of the canal and rattle through the bridgehole with the merest whisker of clearance, moving rapidly into the next length with the following boat shooting the bridge with a "whoosh!"

In the near distance, above the towing path, is the residential district of the Haulgh. The many fine houses backing on to the cut are the homes of the new industrialists and merchants, and it is in one of these properties that the coalowners, the Fletchers, have their home.

We are now quickly coming to the most remarkable feat of canal engineering on the entire length of the Manchester, Bolton and Bury Canal - the aqueduct at Dam Side. This splendid arched construction carries the canal from the high ground of the Haulgh over the deep valley through which the River Croal flows. Along the towing path and on to the 'duct speed the horses, the boat following - what a sensation! We have the feeling that we are flying through the air. We are a terrific height above the river, which can be seen tumbling over its rocky course, and gasps of amazement can be heard along with exclamations of fear from those making the journey for the first time. It is still a little daunting for some of the more experienced amongst us and one man says that he will never get used to this short but unnerving part of the journey, even though the clip-clop of the horses' hooves and the swish of the water along the side do give some little reassurance. The view through the windows is magnificent, and yet it is only one of the many which we shall see on our journey.

Sighs of relief and expressions of thanks greet the sight of land on each side of the canal. There is a group of buildings on the near side (Darcy Lever) and on the far side the river winds away past a farm and several cottages. This village, small though it is, is highly industrialised, and from the boat it is possible to see at once a dozen mine workings – outcrop, declivity entry and shafts with winding gear – all working and all helping to supply the ever-increasing demand for coal.

There is the Hacken Colliery, linked to the canal by a tramway which climbs fifty feet to a loading dock, and a tramway from the Victoria Colliery running downhill for almost two hundred yards to a second loading dock. The countryside has taken on that dead, dull grey, overcast look always attendant on colliery undertakings; the roads are covered with that repulsive, black, clinging sludge which soils everything in the vicinity. The view down the Croal Valley, once one of the most pleasing in Lancashire, has in recent years lost its sparkle. The fresh green of the vegetation is subdued, the watercourses, even in flow, have a film of pollution and the bright sunshine has become overcast by the pall of smoke which issues from the tall chimneys belonging to the several manufacturing concerns which have mushroomed hereabouts since the turn of the century. These industries have, of course, provided fresh sources of employment, and a high rate of pay is attracting people from districts far afield. This is particularly evidenced by the steady increase in house building; it is said that there are schools being started for local children and that there is a move to what some folk call sanitation. There are those people who say that the Croal Valley, small though it is, is playing a very significant part in steering England along the road to

Fogg's Pit   *(J Santley)*

a prosperity far in excess of anything that has ever been known before, but then some folk say lots of things.

As the boat moves on, looking west through the cabin windows and down into the valley we can see the works of John Smith, manufacturer of the acid which is revolutionising the cotton trade in the processing and bleaching of woven cloth. This is a rapidly developing industry and many such chemical works are opening in the locality. Eastwards on the far side of the canal are a number of small colliery workings. For the most part they are owner-managed, not unusual and certainly not a bad thing either. Not many people are employed here and the gross output of coal is not very great; the largest of these workings is Fogg's.

The boat is travelling at a spanking pace and the turn just before the aqueduct at Farnworth Bridge looms ahead. Looking down into the valley where the river makes another wide sweep, we notice on the bend the paper-making mill of Mr John Crompton. At this point of the river a weir has been made to control the flow of water, and in addition several artificial lakes have been constructed for the storage of water, which is a very important ingredient in the manufacture of paper. The Crompton interests are not confined to paper production; weaving, bleaching and even the printing of a newspaper come under their direction. It is said that the son of John, Thomas Bonsor Crompton, acts as financial adviser and often banker to local businessmen. There are many now-prominent local firms which can thank Thomas Bonsor Crompton for the support and advice given in their formative years. To the right of the works stands a very fine house which Mr John Crompton built in the early part of this century. Those with keen eyesight can make out the old pack horse road as it passes the west gable of Rock Hall, as this house is known. Further to the west can be seen the roof and chimneys of Darley Hall.

No sooner are we over the aqueduct than we are passing Farnworth Bridge Colliery and there is a shaft with winding gear very close to the towing path. The horses clatter over a stone bridge, under which is the access to a small harbour. Below, in the valley, is another shaft and winding gear and it is interesting to note that one winding engine house services both shafts. Neither of these pits has been noted for high productivity and in the last few years their main function has been to serve as pumping stations to clear the surplus water from the nearby workings of the Ladyshore Pits.

Across the canal the banking swings away to form a wide basin, a place for unloading boats and a place for mooring boats, known as the "Salt Harbour". It is here that the salt boats out of Northwich and the chemical salt boats out of Runcorn unload their cargoes to be carted to the several paper-making and chemical works in the locality. It will be noticed that the canal banking on both sides is built of stone, and that

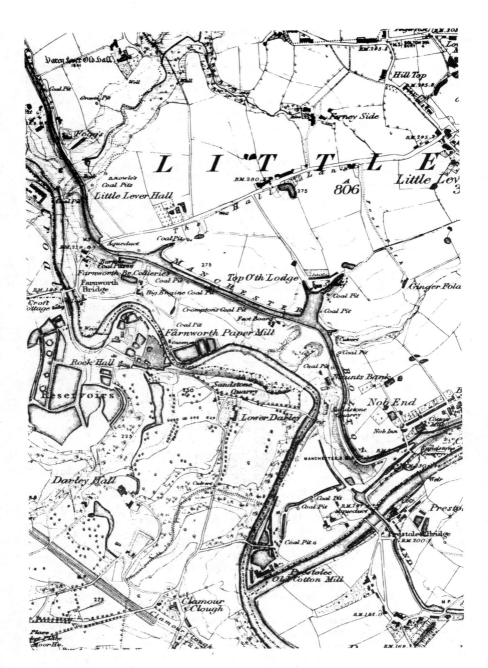

this strength continues for some distance ahead (in fact it continues to well past Ladyshore Colliery). The surface of the harbour banking and the way to the turnpike are paved with setts to give a hard standing for the discharge of cargoes and a good exit.

From here the length is known as the Blue Wall Length, a name derived from a strongly-built wall of blue bricks which extends along the entire stretch. When the canal was being cut the land at this point presented a stability problem and it was realised that the banking would have to be considerably strengthened. So the towing path was made much wider than usual and a retaining wall was taken well below the level of the canal and built on a foundation of rock. The canal is far wider in this length than in most places, a further measure to protect a weak banking, as in the severe weather ice pressure is less in a wider channel than it is in a narrower one.

At the end of the Blue Wall Length the canal takes a right hand turn and just on the turn, on the far side, can be seen the colliery and boatbuilding yard of Andrew Knowles. A short cutting to the north serves this busy site, "Top o'th Lodge". The colliery produces well and the boatbuilding yard turns out craft for the fleet that services the Andrew Knowles group of collieries and also for one or two small canal operators unable to build their own.

By now traffic on the canal is increasing, as we can see by the number of boats with a variety of cargoes and loads coming towards us. It is interesting to guess from which part of the country they hail. Some, as we can easily see, are local, with coal or manufactured goods in large bales from Bury, timber and stone or lime from further afield, and bales of raw cotton from perhaps Liverpool. For as far as we can follow the line of the canal ahead there are boats approaching, and each and every one will give right of way to the Passenger Packet. None can plead that it is unaware of our coming; the horn and the voice of the postilion make sure that they all know.

With a hard shove on the tiller the Captain swings the Packet round the right hand turn and once again we are treated to a panoramic view of the Croal Valley. From this vantage point high above the river can be seen the meeting of the waters of the Croal and Irwell. A number of people on board are saying that this was a beautiful stretch of country not so long ago, before the industry moved here. As we look across the Croal we get another and better view of Darley Hall, and overlooking the river is Darley Farm. There is the old pack horse road skirting the farmyard before it descends to cross the pack horse bridge over the Croal.

On the far side of us the land is high and on a knoll stands a large, gaunt house, a farm called Naunts bank. Indeed, it is a very special farm, the property of the Lansdale family, canal

15

people from the very beginning. Owd Joe o't'Mills did contract carting when the waterway was under construction and has kept an interest since. From the extensive stables horses are hired for work on the canal, and it is also one of several changing posts for the Packet horses. It is a place used by the people engaged in the long distance traffic and over the stables there is a large loft which is used as sleeping accommodation for the men and boys who work these boats. It is also by way of being an employment agency for such people.

Just here there is much to see and our Packet is speeding onwards now to the Canal Company Depot at Nob End. By the towing path is the mason's yard, with masses of stone in varying states of preparation; some, evidently fresh from the quarry, is being unloaded from a moored boat, and in another part of the yard a group of men are dressing large slabs which will be used in the constant maintenance work which the bankings of the canal demand.

The horses have slackened their pace, and as we near the end of the stoneyard they are at a walk. People are bustling about, gathering parcels and the like, and all the time the Packet is losing way. Finally, after gracefully making the turn to the front of the main buildings, the vessel is secured by ready hands to the ring bolts set in the coping stones verging the canal. The banking is paved for the entire area of the depot, which is the Company post at the northern end of the Manchester, Bolton and Bury Canal. From this centre all the maintenance work for the greater part of the waterway is done. We have just passed the mason's yard and the building now to our front, on the left near the wicket gate, is the office, staffed by a clerk who in addition to his general duties sells tickets to the travelling public. There is also the office of the District Superintendent; very rarely will he be found behind his desk as he is a practical man who is always about on some job in hand.

Adjoining the offices is the large and spacious carpenters' shop. The massive lock gates are made and repaired here, along with the hundred and one other carpentry jobs which the canal requires. Next door is the boatbuilders' shop, opening on to a wide area of hardstanding. It is on to this space that the Company's boats are hauled for repair. To one side of the "hard" is the oven or steamer which is used for treating the planking when such repair work is being carried out. On the far side and to the rear of the boatbuilders' cabin is the blacksmith's shop, always a very busy place in any maintenance depot on the canal. If we look to our right and beyond the "hard", a neat cottage is visible with a sign stating that refreshments are available there and a well-kept garden furnished with small tables and seating is to be seen by the side. Further to our right is a large house in a walled garden, the residence of the foreman in charge of the stonemason's gang. The Houldsworth family, father and son, have held this post since the canal was built and they have lived in this same house.

This is the Nob Depot, clean and well looked after, as all the Company establishments are kept to the very high standard which the management require.

Not only the depot takes our interest, for here is the junction of the Bolton and Bury length with the staircase of locks which carries the waterway to the lower level and on to Manchester. The locks, a staircase of six - two flights of three with a pound in the middle - are overlooked by the lockkeeper's cottage with the usual offices. This is a busy flight of locks perched on the side of the steep valley through which the River Irwell flows.

Nob End, the hamlet which gives name to this area, is a thriving place. It has in the region of thirty dwellings, two pubs, a chapel, two coal pits (even though they are of the one-egg standard) and a cotton mill owned by T B Crompton. There are two servants from the Nob Inn on the landing stage in front of the offices, selling ale from jugs.

All those passengers who are bound for Manchester have left the Packet Boat and are making their way to the wicket gate at the end of the landing; those who are en route for Bury remain where they are. A number of people who have been waiting at the depot intending to make the trip to Bury are now getting aboard with help and encouragement from the local dock porters.

Having passed through the wicket gate, we make our way down a very steep pathway, which is covered against the weather, and runs between the rear of the depot and the locks. To those who have not made this trip before the changing of boats seems odd, but there is very good reason. The conservation of water is a major factor in any canal operation and the working of the locks costs many thousands of gallons, so to minimise such a loss the Packet Boats ask their patrons to walk the short distance under cover and with the least inconvenience, assisted with their parcels and packages by the willing dock porters, to the lower level where another smart Packet and fresh horses wait to continue the journey.

The basin at the foot of the locks is not in the most salubrious of settings. Here is a highly industrial area on a triangle formed by the flood plain at the confluence of the rivers Croal and Irwell. At the base of this triangle is the chemical works of Benjamin Rawson, manufacturer of the new product, vitriol, an acid now so widely used in the bleaching of cloth. The manufacture of vitriol has an adverse effect on the immediate surrounding area; vegetation is stunted and turning black, stonework and brickwork are the same and the air is filled with evil-smelling fumes.

Whilst the canal was in the final stages of construction, Benjamin Rawson transferred his business interests from the Halliwell district of Bolton to this site, which offered many facilities, being in close proximity to the new transport system, and having its own coal supply in the shape of two mine workings. A further advantage was that it was on the fringe of the two rapidly expanding cotton manufacturing districts of Farnworth and Prestolee. The apex of the triangle gives access to a bridge at the foot of a steep hill and a paved road leading up towards Farnworth.

North from the basin, at the foot of the locks, is a spur, or short canal, extending for about three hundred yards before turning sharply to the west. There is a boatbuilding yard with a dry dock, which by manipulating a sluice gate discharges its water into the River Croal; a very unusual feature for the local boat yards. Along this same spur are the warehouses and wharves for the dispatch and receipt of cargoes; to the rear of these buildings and more to the centre of the triangle are the offices and the stabling for the large number of horses used here.

In less than fifteen minutes we have all made our way from the wicket gate down the covered pathway, boarded the Packet Boat, stowed away parcels, packages, bundles, boxes and crates and settled ourselves to continue the journey to Manchester.

Once again the Captain's horn sounds, the horse handlers ease their charges into the collar and the boat, helped by the barge poles of the dockers, is under way. The mounted postilion cracks his whip, the horses are now moving at a smart pace and are encouraged into a run by the shouting of the mounted man. (Wherever do they find these leather-lunged, raucous-voiced people? Possibly they grow them.) The smart passenger boat hauled by well-groomed horses is away on the second leg of the passage to Manchester, over the aqueduct which crosses the Irwell and along the wide length to the turn which gives sight of the village of Prestolee, and all the time the oncoming traffic gives way to our Packet Boat.

The village of Prestolee is set in a semi-rural area which has strong connections with the cotton trade, particularly with handloom weaving. Recently several cotton mills have come into existence and there is also paper making on a reasonable scale. Just over the River Irwell (the Croal Valley has now become the Irwell Valley) are the coalmine workings of Kearsley, making the district a pleasantly prosperous one. This neighbourhood also has strong religious connections, in contrast to other places in the locality.

We are making good time through the outskirts of Prestolee and it is noticeable that the volume of the oncoming traffic is not quite so heavy. Not very far ahead are the locks at Ringley and these, like any other locks, tend to thin out the number of

18

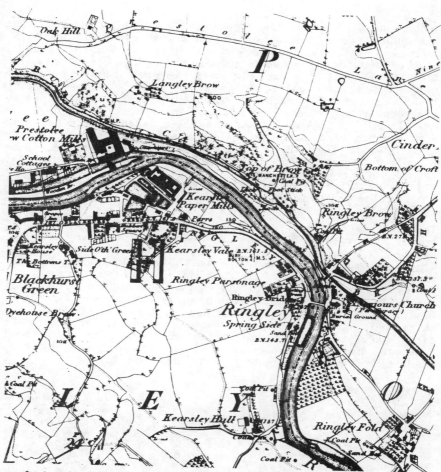

craft in the vicinity. But those boats that are approaching us, no matter what their cargoes, drop their lines and, in accordance with the Company's bylaw, give us the "inside". Through all this our postilion handles his charges with such efficiency and skill that neither the step nor the speed falters. The rattle of the shod hooves, the shouting of the postilion and the happy-handed sounding of the horn by the Captain keep all and sundry aware of the approach of the important Packet Boat and when Ringley Bridge Lock comes into view it can be seen that the gates are open ready to receive us.

There is a flight of two locks here – a single lock, a pound and a second lock. The speed of the horses has now dropped to a walk; our agile Captain has hopped from his place on the stern on to the towing path and having put a rope on the timber head, he is now bending it round a bollard. The dismounted postilion is doing the same with the lead line at the for'd end. All way has now been taken off and the boat is almost stopped; the nimble postilion quickly steps from the towing path on to the deck, unhooks the lines from the ringbolts and steps ashore again. The sweating horses are now standing thankfully by the railings which fringe the towing path, grabbing a few minutes rest, whilst the boat is lowered to the next length. Not quite all way has been taken off the boat and with the aid of a barge pole it is eased into the lock and the gates closed. The sluice paddle is lifted part way, and the postilion, having coiled his lines, moves his beasts to the far end of the second lock where there is a small patch of rough grass which the horses can nibble until they are needed again. The lockkeeper and his wife (or is it his daughter?) stand ready at the outlet gates.

The passengers, even those who have several trips to their credit, are seeking positions of advantage; some are standing in the well before the for'd deck, others are in the stern, whilst the more venturesome are risking the Captain's rebuke by scrambling on to the roof of the cabins – hallowed ground, not for the likes of passengers. But everyone is anxious "Fer t'miss nowt". The Captain stands strong and silent on the fore deck, having but a short time before done his usual two hops, two skips and a very long jump to get from the stern, across the cabin roof, to the nose end of the boat. There he waits, boat hook in hand, for the water level in the lock to drop sufficiently for his vessel to pass to the lower length.

Ringley Locks   *(Swinton Library)*

Entering and leaving a lock is an operation requiring expertise; under no circumstances must the boat foul the gates, nor must the sluice paddle tongues be damaged by inconsiderate working. The slightest damage would disrupt the entire canal system for a considerable time and probably lose an irreplaceable amount of precious water, a catastrophe in the dry season.

As we reach the lower level the lockkeeper assists in hooking up and getting the horses moving. On this occasion the pace is a steady walk, because a few hundred yards from the exit of the lock the canal takes a turn to the left, then swings in a wide loop to pass the rear of the Horse Shoe public house, a scheduled stop for all Manchester-bound Packets. We take aboard passengers here, parcels are left for local delivery and are taken for places further on the journey. As all this is time-consuming, the landlord gladly serves ale to the thirsty and to those who do not need an excuse to quaff a tankard of foaming beer. It would be difficult to get a nicer day for this trip; warm sunshine with just a breath of a breeze from the south. Many of the male travellers have removed their coats and the lady passengers would no doubt like to do the same, but decorum rules no. The length of canal ahead is straight, a number of pairs of boats are coming towards us - but there is something else. Noses twitch, and again, looks are exchanged and there is some bewilderment. Someone explodes: "Phew! What th'ell?" He is reassured by the Captain: "Nothing to worry about, sir. Only the night soil from Salford and Manchester. At this time, or near enough, every day, farmers go mad for it." Looking around at the fertile fields with fine crops in evidence, it is a fact not to be doubted.

A few more minutes and the night soil boats pass by. We get a wave from the very healthy looking woman at the tiller of the rear boat. Then they have gone and all that lingers is an aroma. "Let's 'ave moor ale fer t'shift yon stink!" is the almost general call and it is noticed that even the clerical gentlemen are not abstaining this time.

The extra delay is not more than a few moments, but it is a matter of pride and good timekeeping that the loss be made good. The Captain is now rather impatient and irritably calls: "All aboard, if you please!" The postilion is already mounted and the local horse handler is holding the bridle of the lead horse. "Come on, get a move on, will yer?" the tardy ones amongst the travellers are urged. The light breeze has cleared the "aroma" and on this fine summer morning the Horse Shoe, with its attractive setting, is a hard place to leave - especially as "Th'ale's so good". So it is with a show of reluctance that our travelling companions resume their places in the boat.

The horn sounds, the postilion is as usual shouting his head off and cracking his whip as though there was no tomorrow; the ostler calmly eases the mettlesome horses forward to take the

21

strain in the collars and our boat is once again on the move. Free from the ostler's control, the two horses pick up speed and in a remarkably short distance are at the run. Thrusting the tiller hard over, the Captain manoeuvres his craft to the midstream and swings gracefully round the turn into the next length. The historic Church of St Saviours seems to glide past, the churchyard wall forming the boundary to the towing path.

No sooner is the church left behind than the canal enters a wooded region; the density of the trees and thick foliage subdues the morning sunshine, but one has the feeling that the valley is widening and the occasional flash of silver from the river confirms that it is going further away.

We are now travelling a length which is straight for as far as we can see and although the woodland continues on each side there are places where the trees thin out. Not clearings as such, but it is possible to see more and further. Travelling through the woods can be rather an eerie experience; the half-light of subdued green, the closeness of the trees acts as a blanket to sound, the earthen towing path deadens the thud of the shod hooves and even the ripple of the water past the bows is but a whisper. There is no birdsong, the bellowing postilion is strangely quiet and the buzz of chatter amongst the passengers has stilled. Is it a little colder all of a sudden or is it a feeling of apprehension which is the cause of the slight shiver? Fortunately the woods are clearing a little and we can see the cottage at Giant's Seat Lock out in the open in the distance. "Heigh up, wot's this 'ere?" The canal emerges into a clearing and has widened considerably. On the far side is a loading stage, obviously a coal wharf, but in such an unexpected place.

Giant's Seat Lock
(F Sunderland)

Outwood Colliery, which is situated high on the rim of the valley wall about a mile and a half from the canal, obviously does not have immediate access to this greatly improved mode of transport. A waggon road has been made from the pit head across country, down the side

22

of the valley to the canal side and a wharf and loading stages have been built, thereby affording an outlet to the hungry Manchester market. The waggons are operated by horses and by steam winches in the manner common nowadays in such circumstances.

The loading place is no sooner alongside than it has slipped astern and our attention is taken by the locks which are coming up. The horn and/or the postilion – there's not much to choose between them – are not on this occasion needed as a warning system. We are expected. Can it be that the lockkeeper has a timepiece or is it because the Packet arrives at the same time every day? The fact remains that we are awaited, the gates of the lock are open to receive us, the horses slow and then stop. Once again as if by magic the Captain appears on the small foredeck, barge pole firmly in hand, and the dismounted horseman, having looped a short line on the for'd timber head, is now running the rope round a bollard on the lock side. The same is being done by the lockkeeper at the stern end. "Steady, steady, STEADY!" instructs the Captain. The way is now almost off the vessel, the restraining ropes are removed from the bollards and taken to another set closer to the lock gates; two tree-stump-like posts set into the banking on either side of the approach to the lock ensure that the boats always enter the lock without way and under hand control.

We are now in the lock and the gates are closed on us. Short lines from the boat to the short metal bollards on the coping keep the craft still, the towing lines have been cast ashore and the lockkeeper and his wife work the winches controlling the sluice paddles, easing the tongues slightly at first. The ropes from the timberheads to the shore bollards are removed, the water level in the lock begins to drop and the boat sinks down with it.

Locking takes some little time and to those people not actively engaged in the work, it can, after the first experience, be rather a bore. However, we are fortunate that Giant's Seat is such an interesting place and there is so much for the traveller to see. Set as it is in the fold of the valley, Giant's Seat is considered to be one of the local beauty spots and it is not surprising that pleasure boat excursions make this one of several focal points for trips in the summer season. There is a notice board advertising that teas are served here and to the rear of the cottage, to the east, we see an extensive meadow fringed by a well-wooded valley side – an ideal picnic area. Southwards, in the direction of Manchester, is the widening view of the Irwell flood plain. To the west is another wooded area extending up the far side of the valley wall to the ridge; the green of the foliage makes an attractive backdrop to this lovely rural setting and through the trees a flash of silver indicates the River Irwell.

The lockkeeper's cottage is on an artificial island which fronts the lock. A short distance before the lock gates, on the Ringley side, is a weir over which the excess water in that length is run into a stone lined pound at the far side of the building. (This excess water is drainage from the high ground to the east which flanks the canal all the way along this valley.) On the south end of this pound is a second weir which controls the flow of water into a wide basin at the exit of the lower lock.

Across the basin and at a slightly higher level is Giant's Seat House. In front of this fine building but on the canal level is a dry dock, used as a sub depot by the Canal Company. A permanent workforce is not kept here; it is used as and when requirements dictate.

Canal operators who have travelled considerable distances and are from other navigations use the basin as a tying-up place of a night and make use of the large stable facilities at Giant's Seat House. Some of the larger hauling companies, such as Pickford's, who I am told conduct a carrying service which covers the entire inland waterway system of the country, keep one horse here permanently in case a replacement is required. The Passenger Packet Service too avail themselves of this facility.

Back to the lockkeeper's cottage. The cellar of this building is so fitted out that overnight accommodation is readily available for a number of people, should it be required; we have here a canal-side guest house.

Whilst we have been taking in all the interesting features of the locality, making several inspections and absorbing the information concerning the facilities available, the Packet Boat has passed through the locks and entered the basin. Now we are being urged in no uncertain manner to "rejoin the ship" and we move, perhaps reluctant once again to leave an attractive place on a lovely summer's morning. As a number of us make our way from the top lock, the Captain shouts, "Please make haste, gentlemen!" "'Ee means ger a bloody move on," one of my fellow travellers remarks. So we do.

We hardly have time to scramble aboard; the Packet is already on the move, the horn sounds deafeningly as we run alongside and some of us make a rather undignified spectacle nipping with varying degrees of agility from the coping to the boat.

The Packet is now well under way, moving at a spanking pace, and only the sounds of the horses and the creak of their gear disturb the morning stillness. From far ahead comes the faint sound of a horn. It is the morning Packet out of Oldfield Road en route for Bolton. The Captain noticeably bristles – there is a good deal of friendly rivalry between the several Packet boats, the masters and crews, so it is a matter of pride that compels him to demonstrate that he commands a smartly-run vessel and that his crew know their business. Making a wide, sweeping turn, our Packet, Manchester bound, enters the length which will bring us next to Rhodes Lock.

The woods between the canal and the river are now thinning and the attention of fellow passengers who have not previously made this journey is attracted to another interesting feature. Looking west, the river runs very close to the towing path and across the river can be seen another canal; from the type of boats which are using it there is an obvious connection with a colliery. This is "Fletcher's Sough", which extends from below Giant's Seat to Clifton Aqueduct.

Forty years ago Matthew Fletcher, pioneer, in fact the instigator of this waterway on which we are travelling, had under his control two collieries; Wet Earth and Botany Bay. Neither had a good record of production because both were bedevilled by excess water in the workings. Fletcher employed the engineer James Brindley to provide a method of mine drainage worked on the waterwheel principle: river water is diverted through a tunnel and works the mechanism before returning to the river – a very ingenious and very successful undertaking. A second problem which at that time was causing concern to Matthew Fletcher was transport, particularly between his two coal pits. A length of canal was cut and the drainage from the two mines was used to water this navigation. When the main canal was built in 1795 "Fletcher's Sough" was connected to it by a shallow lock hard by Clifton Aqueduct.

The relatively short distance between the basin at Giant's Seat and Rhodes Lock is quickly covered, and once again our horses are slackening speed and our Captain makes his appearance on the deck. Now we are again in the familiar process of locking.

I have already mentioned the holiday excursions which are made with unfailing regularity to this lovely part of the Irwell Valley; in fact the term "beautiful" would be no exaggeration. It is a jewel in a splendid setting and it is difficult to believe that such rural charm can be found cheek by jowl with industrial development; but then Lancashire has always been known for its pleasant and attractive places.

Giant's Seat, Margaret Barlow's Tea Gardens and Rhodes Lock, all within this locality, attract hundreds of trippers at weekends and holidays in the summer. Each offers the pleasure-seekers recreational facilities of one form or another – refreshments, picnic spots and plenty of room for games or for walking. Margaret Barlow's speciality is advertised – "Egg Teas" – and these can be partaken of in the very nice gardens or in the clean eating rooms in the house. For those who have come to picnic, jugs of tea will be provided, or even hot water for "them uz wants brew their own". The surrounding country has several things to offer. A nearby fold in the ground forms a saucer-like depression which is filled by a spring of the purest water that it is possible to find anywhere in the country and this is used as an open-air swimming pool. The meadow land round about is a popular camping ground.

Over towards the river and across it we can see the Wet Earth Colliery, and ahead towards the south in the near distance is Botany Bay.

Locking at Rhodes does not take as long as previously, there being just one lock. From ahead comes the sound of a horn and perhaps from the instinct of one animal answering another we are treated to a blast on our own horn; or is it because we are again well under way with the horses giving of their best?

The attention of the passengers is now very much divided. There is the activity of the colliery scenes as they glide past on the right hand side and the approaching but so far unseen Packet from Manchester. All at once several voices proclaim: "There it is!" and round the far turn appear the running horses, followed by the boat. The combined speeds of the converging boats bring them quickly towards each other. What a brave sight – the running horses almost charging us, their postilion cracking his whip above his head and uttering almost fiendish noises, the smart-looking Packet boat with a shining scythe blade mounted on the bow and glinting wickedly in the morning sunshine, the polished brasswork, gleaming paints and sparkling of the polished windows, the freshly pipe-clayed ropework and the faces of passengers looking intently forward as though at their own reflection in an enormous mirror. The Bolton Packet on which we are travelling presents exactly the same picture to

Rhodes Lock   *(Swinton Library)*

those who are speeding towards us and as we watch the horses of the approaching boat slow and then stop, lines are unhooked and the Packet yaws wide, allowing our boat the uninterrupted passage on the inside – the code of courtesy on "t'cut". Our Packet will return the compliment later in the day when on the journey from Manchester to Bolton. Once they have passed each other, the distance between the two boats increases so fast that the Packet far astern is no longer of interest to our fellow passengers. Once again the events nearer to us take our attention. The two canals are on a parallel course and Fletcher's is alive with a traffic all of its own; the Botany Bay pit is now well astern of us, and that other cut looks as though it is coming closer. "If thee opp'ns thi' ees thel see it is." "Aye, thet reet, thet noan rung." The buildings which are the centres of activity can now be plainly seen and made out to be sawmills. Beside them there are saw pits, vast stacks of timber, sawn planks and logs, a large covered boat dock with a wide area of hard standing big enough to take several boats, a smithy which looks to be unusually busy with its several forges roaring away, a line of loaded coal boats tied two abreast and the inevitable stacks of coal. Men and boys and some women too are hurrying to and fro in this lively scene of industry.

When Matthew Fletcher saw that his projected Manchester, Bolton & Bury Canal was not only a fact but also a viable commercial undertaking, he lost no time in turning it to his best advantage. The boatbuilding and sawing facilities belonged to him and many canal users who do not have building yards of their own buy Fletcher-built craft. The products of the Clifton yards can be found on most of the waterways of the country's canal system, even as far distant as London. The timber, particularly sawn, is in great demand locally and in his way Matthew Fletcher has provided employment for a very large number of people where it did not exist before, at wages far in excess of anything they had previously known. He is deserving of the most grateful thanks, but there are those who begrudge his enterprise.

Now the two canals and the river seem to be coming together and we are at Clifton Aqueduct. Fletcher's Sough rises by a single shallow lock to the level of the main canal, which is carried over the river by an aqueduct of single boat width, through a low roving bridge. The horses are uncoupled and walked over the bridge, the towing path changes from our right hand side to our left and in this same direction the canal makes a turn. Recoupling the horses is only a matter of minutes and we are soon on our way again, travelling as quickly as before.

The Packet has a refreshment service aboard and a comely female presides over a small compartment at the rear of the Second Class cabin in which there is fixed a small stove. On the morning boats a breakfast can be purchased and several times in the course of the journey two pretty girls offer cakes and sweetmeats from baskets to the passengers, just as they are doing at this moment, and they would seem to be making good trade, too. Those people who partook of breakfast paid one shilling; cakes and the like are tuppence, mugs of tea are available for those who wish such refreshment and in addition the now very popular lemonade is on sale during this hot weather and very welcome it is.

The River Irwell, we notice, has made a very wide loop to the east but we can still follow its course through a colourful outcrop of red sandstone once again. This same feature has occurred at points along the course of the Irwell, with one very much in evidence at Radcliffe, and we wonder if this is the same stratum of rock.

The valley is now widening out into a plain and in the distance ahead a haze of smoke, a church tower here and a steeple there indicate that we are at last nearing the end of our journey. The traffic in both directions is certainly more numerous and of a greater variety than before, with cargoes of cotton, wool, stone, bricks and building materials, lime, chemical salts, milk and pottery − if it is made in England it will be seen on the canal. Each and every boat as usual dips

Bridge over the Bolton Canal, 1888

28

its lines and gives the inside passage to the superior Packet boat.

We are now at a very interesting part of the canal and we can see that the passageway is much wider than we have generally sailed through and that both bankings are built of dressed stone. In fact the whole is a stone trough to a depth of nine to ten feet of water, which is of a much darker shade, affected most likely by the land drainage hereabouts – the appearance is somewhat sinister.

The wide sweep followed by the Irwell has taken it out of our sight, but the far valley wall can still be seen and the wide flood plain which lies between us and the river is well developed farmland and continues so for as far as we can see ahead. There are well tended fields with good crops, made possible, no doubt, by the ample supply of night soil from the nearby towns.

A stone marker on the far side of the towing path informs us that we are $3\frac{3}{4}$ miles from our destination, the horn is sounded regularly now and the traffic is even thicker than before. Agecroft Bridge is coming up; we shall put passengers ashore here and perhaps take on several more; parcels will no doubt be unloaded and others put on board. This will be the pattern at the stopping places before we come to the terminus at Oldfield Road. We pass through Agecroft Bridge and though the paved path dips sharply as it goes under, the horses do not even change step. On the other side of the bridge there is nobody waiting to board the Packet, none of our passengers intends to land here, there are no parcels to take on nor any to put ashore; it is not often that this happens at Agecroft.

Bending to the right, the canal enters a long straight length of very wide construction. It is not of the "trough" principle here, nor is it, so far as we can see, for a long way ahead. On each side of the waterway we have open agricultural land.

On the towing path side, in an easterly direction, the land is well tended and in the middle distance is Kersal Hall, a pleasantly situated half-timbered building, the original structure dating to Saxon times. This property has a very colourful history and is the subject of some hair-raising and lurid legends. The least bloody and perhaps most entertaining of these states that Kersal Hall has the distinction of being the house into which tea was first introduced in England. A son of the Langleys, the family who were then resident, served in the Navy early in the seventeenth century and when visiting China he sent home a jar of "chaw", together with a note describing it as being highly esteemed by the Chinese. But he gave no instructions as to how it should be used or prepared and the people at the Hall thought it must be some kind of vegetable and cooked it as such, draining off the liquid and serving the boiled leaves; they did not like it one little bit! Another member of the same

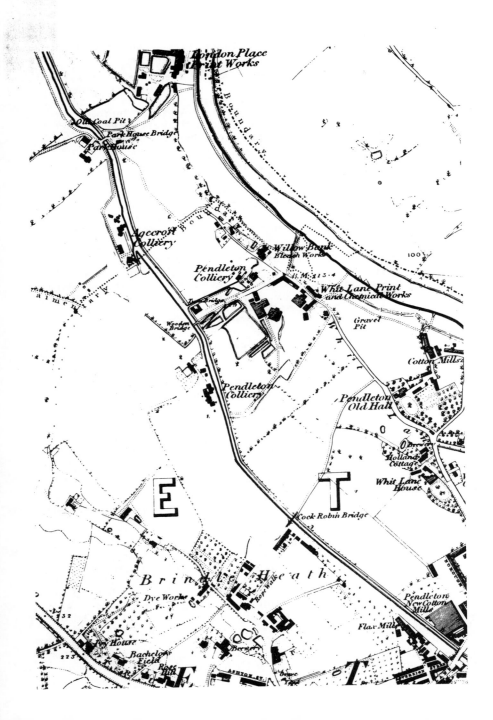

family is credited with the introduction of clogs to Lancashire. In Kersal Vale we see good land under cultivation. It is a summer day as fine and warm as it could be, with sunshine and a bright blue sky, yet despite this there is a feeling of unease, a very slight chill, as though a cold breath has touched our warm flesh. Through the ages Kersal has had such an effect on people. Into our line of vision comes Kersal Cell, another building of Saxon origin, although some say it may date from even earlier. Over the centuries it has alternated as a private residence and as the centre of a religious order of one kind or another, the changes being many and often. It has a long and chequered history, bloody and supernatural, as has the Hall, and we experience a slight relief at having these buildings astern.

The gently wooded section which now takes our attention has a pleasing aspect even though the sudden change from farmland to woodland is rather unexpected. The land between the canal and the distant river is a fine and very extensive orchard which produces abundant crops of a standard equal to the products of any orchard in the length and breadth of our country.

The frequency and weight of the canal traffic is now very noticeable, boats loaded with coal predominating. We can now see pithead gear, the far banking is again stone-built and there is the entrance to a loading harbour; there are boats under chutes which, it would seem, are able to load two or three at one time. The loaded ones then go forward and rejoin the canal proper by the harbour exit, to be moored on the far

Kersal Hall   *(Salford Local History Library)*

Colliery in Irwell Valley   *(Swinton Library)*

side of the canal until they make the trip to Salford or maybe further afield. This then is Agecroft Colliery, one of several which belong to Andrew Knowles.

The canal is still very deep hereabouts and the Captain has just said to me that it will continue so right into Salford. The orchards again take our attention; the fruit can be clearly seen and the harvest in a month or two should be very good indeed. Most of the crop will be transported by canal boats to points far and wide and to towns that now enjoy a better standard of living because of this new form of transport for their food supplies.

From here the way to Salford is almost a straight line. The view over the country to the west is obscured at the moment by the high ground on that side but on the towing path side it can be seen that the valley plain is broadening and that cultivation is very much in evidence. This district between Kersal and Salford, at least through Pendleton, is rightly regarded these days as the market garden of the rapidly expanding industrial centres of this part of Lancashire.

So far the speed of our journey has been marked, but we have now to proceed at a slower pace because of the density of traffic and the frequency of the halts. The horn blasts are almost continuous. The negotiation of a way through the heavy traffic makes the Captain's expertise evident; his ability in steering can not be doubted. The general atmosphere, which a short time ago was very relaxed, is now noticeably tense and the passengers are showing signs of the approaching end of their journey, making sure that packages and parcels or bundles are to hand. Travelling companions who in the course of the trip have become inadvertently separated (or otherwise) are now seeking each other out and the bolder ones (and there are some) are hastily making assignations for the return journey to Bolton this evening.

The horses are stopping, the Packet eases into the wharf, some goods are unloaded for collection by the local carrier and the onward passage is resumed. The next stop will be the one which in the racing season is the point of disembarkation for many excursions carrying large numbers of sporting ladies and gentlemen, their destination the racecourse at Castle Irwell, some short walking distance downhill towards Broughton. Today those people who have business in this fine village will leave the boat at this point.

The orchards have now given way to a soft fruit growing area specialising in strawberries, cherries, blackcurrants and goose-berries. This sort of cultivation is in turn replaced by a vast rose garden, where bushes yield some of the most attractive of those typically English blooms, and then this beautiful garden gives way to fine houses in their own small parklands, the residences of the ever-growing numbers of leaders of industry and business in the rapidly expanding town of Salford.

We are now at Frederick Road Bridge and the wharf of that name is in sight as soon as the Packet has shot through. Many of our fellow passengers are going ashore and the halt here is of longer duration than at any other stopping place since Ringley.

As we leave Frederick Road the outlook changes quickly, almost suddenly. From the pleasant aspect of orchards and rose gardens we are thrust into the harsher realities of the means of earning a living – wharves, yards and warehouses are now on both banks of the canal. There is a variety of merchandise; coal is of course predominant, with timber either in logs or sawn planking, raw cotton and wool, bolts of cloth and bundles of piece goods. Boats are discharging a cargo of kits of milk, and others are landing farm produce. There are loads of freshly-ground flour in sacks, ingots of iron for the foundry, once again we see the salt boats from Northwich and there are several passing us now loaded with chemicals, no doubt out of Runcorn and bound perhaps for those works we saw in the Croal Valley. Over there is a boat from Staffordshire with its cargo of pottery and we are now in the Windsor Bridge length. As a depot for merchandise, Windsor Bridge is second only to the main one at Oldfield Road.

The bricklayers' trowels are never still in this town of Salford. On every journey the regular travellers remark on the changes and additions since they were last here. A little to the rear of the depot is a newly erected building: "Sithee, un wot dust caw yon?" is the question. It is another new venture, a brewery, and since it is situated close to the canal the owner has been given permission to draw off water for brewing purposes by means of a two inch pipe. He has, of course, to pay for this privilege, but the Canal Company have, out of consideration, passed a bylaw making it an offence to deposit refuse and the bodies of animals or other repulsive matter in the canal in the vicinity of Windsor Bridge.

Here the canal makes the form of an "S" bend and Windsor Bridge is on the inside of a shallow turn; it is the last main stop before the end of our journey at Oldfield Road and, as is to be expected, many of our companions go ashore and none join us. The canal passes under the Manchester turnpike very close to the top of Cross Lane and there are those who claim that this is the new heart of Salford. Be that as it may, we leave this hive of activity to make our way to the Packet terminus. The scene changes yet again; the yards and staithes are replaced by the new cotton mills, the iron works and printing and dyeing works all going full blast and there is a multitude of canal craft plying to and fro, loading and unloading. Having discharged a cargo at one mill wharf the boats move on to another in search of a fresh load. Tally clerks are buzzing about like flies, or should it be fleas?

Some people may well ask, "Wheer's aw' that lot gooin'?" Perhaps along the Duke of Bridgewater's canal to more than one place: it could be to Northwich, Runcorn, Liverpool, Stoke, Birmingham or anywhere in the Midlands; it could be to Bristol or even to London – so far ranging is the network of inland waterways and Lancashire pioneered it.

There are two locks to be negotiated, but the passengers are not as interested in the process as they were at the start of the trip. They are most anxious to see the end of the journey and to be about the business which brought them here. But it is a different matter with the Captain and the postilion; they are on their mettle, for at this locking the critical and watchful eyes of the experts will be on them – the eyes of men as skilled in canal craft as they are themselves.

The locking is done meticulously, without doubt meeting the approval of the supervising experts, and the Packet boat slides easily into a straight length. Off to the left is a wharf and warehouse area as busy as any we have seen; we pass this and take the next turn sharply to the left. Again there is an area of wharf and warehouse but this time with a difference; this is the Oldfield Road Depot, the terminus for this Packet on which we have travelled. It is clean and tidy on the wharf, where a party of Company people await our arrival – we have journeyed on a most important vessel and its passengers are regarded by the Company as very important people, each and every one of us.

Under a low bridge we go, into a short length and to a landing stage. Willing hands take our ropes and make fast and our Captain is there to help the passengers ashore. The postilion, our whipcracking expert of the fog-horn voice, is as cocky as ever, giving instructions in no uncertain mannner to the stable lads as they lead away the sweating horses to be fed, groomed and rested in readiness for their next journey.

The disembarking passengers are helped ashore by porters who willingly assist further by collecting parcels and packs. It takes some people a little time to find their land legs after a long journey but there is plenty of seating available. The time is nine o'clock on a bright sunny morning, and as some people have not left the boat since the start of the three hour journey, calls must be made urgently.

The hustle and bustle of the landing stage is surveyed by a man resplendent in frock coat and top hat. He is the wharf-master, bidding a welcome to the travellers, a smile here, a word to the regular users of the service, "Good journey?" to one or two, and nods to a great many more he does not recognise as having seen before.

Parcels and packages are soon cleared from the landing; those for the local carriers are sorted to one section and those which are destined to go further afield placed in another. These are

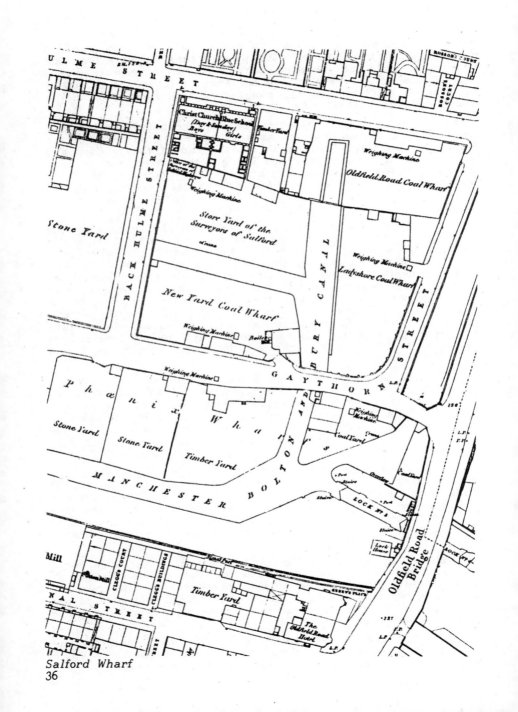

Salford Wharf
36

again sorted to be loaded into the boats which will be most convenient to their delivery. On this landing there are offices and storerooms belonging to Messrs Pickford, the carriers whose service virtually covers the entire country.

The landing stage is soon clear of passengers, the horses have gone and the towing lines have been neatly coiled and placed on the for'd deck of the Packet. The Captain has made his report to the Traffic Superintendent and now several women are cleaning the boat from stem to stern in readiness for the return to Bolton later in the day. The inside of the cabins must be swept and dusted and, if need be, washed; the brasswork made to shine again and the same with the paintwork; the windows receive attention inside and out and the whole turnout must be spick and span, as required by Company policy.

As usual the outward trip has been without problems and the Captain has received the thanks and congratulations of many passengers as they came ashore. But he has now disappeared and as we look round for this worthy man our attention is taken by a large sign at the entrance to a wharf in the far side of the cut. It reads "Ladyshore Coal Wharf", the Salford depot of the Ladyshore Coal Company of Little Lever. This is the destination of the coal we saw being loaded at the loading stages just after we left the Horse Shoe at Ringley.

The Captain is not to be seen and our inquiries elicit the information that most likely he is in the nearby Canal Tavern. "This weather don't 'arf give yer a dry throat. Mine's like sand, sir. Most like the Captain's gone fer a pint, sir. Under the influence of drink? Not the Captain, sir, no, sir. Dead against Company policy that is, sir."

"Postilion, sir? Gone to see to his animals, he has, sir, and then, sir - was he sober when you got here, sir? You thought so, sir? Then he will have gone for several pints, sir. A thirsty job he has, sir, just like mine. Company policy? They don't give a damn if he's sober or not; riding like he does - it's a thirsty job, and so is mine, sir. Oh, thank you kindly, sir. I don't mind if I do; me throat's that dry with talking. Where, sir? Why the Canal Tavern, it's a good place, sir. They sell ale from that new brewery at Windsor Bridge, sir."

PART TWO

WORKING AT LADYSHORE

Whilst the canal was still under construction the Company had to face the question of who would operate it. They realised that a fair sized staff would be required to make the new project efficient and the list of "grades" was a long one; there would be prospects of lifetime employment for those who got the jobs. There were superintendents, clerks, craftsmen of all trades, carters, ostlers, dock labourers, warehousemen, boaters and their lads, maintenance gangs of labourers, puddlers and dredgers, as well as the hangers-on who had no specific designation but who filled in on the hundred and one jobs that came up from time to time.

Canal people were in the beginning recruited from the builders, the more stable and less itinerant of this workforce who, in their many capacities, were to control the staffing and the operating of the waterways for as long as this industry existed. For generations, families controlled boatbuilding, carpentry, stonemasonry and so on. Their rights were very jealously guarded - son followed father and often the same families succeeded to the same job for as many as five or perhaps six generations. Strangers and interlopers were certainly not encouraged.

It was in this way that I came to be one of the canal people. I was the last of five generations of boatbuilders at Ladyshore Coal Company; my people had been there as foremen since the shafts had been sunk, and the Watersons were very much a part of the Ladyshore scene.

I left school at Christmas 1930, when jobs were not easy to come by, and for the first part of 1931 I was looking for work. My father, who was foreman boatbuilder at Ladyshore, said from time to time, "Come with me," but my mother did not want me to go, and I had other ideas myself. My hopes were centred around being a butcher, as my mother's family were in that line of business and I had seen much of it as I had grown up, having been closer to my mother's people than to my father's. However, after a summer of helping out, it was decided that my father should have his way and that I should begin an apprenticeship in the boatdock. Whilst my forebears had seen the canal built, watched it develop into a thriving industry and had taken an active part in all of it, I witnessed the rapid decline and eventual demise of the Manchester, Bolton & Bury Canal.

So it was on an August day in 1931 that I set out for the

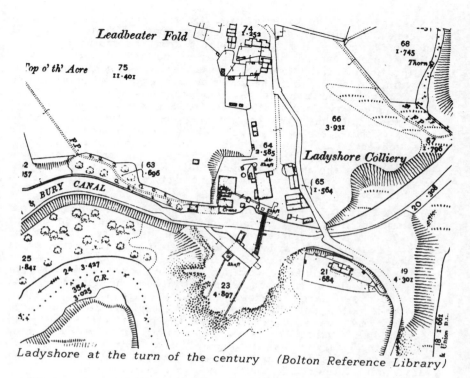

Ladyshore at the turn of the century (Bolton Reference Library)

colliery to see if the manager would take me on. We lived on the west side of Farnworth and it was a long walk through the town, down Peel Street, into and along Cemetery Road, where my grandparents lived, turning down the steep Wilson's Brow to cross the River Croal by the iron bridge at the bottom. Once across I took the path over the Vat Waste, that bleak stretch between the Croal and the foot of Nob End Locks where the now rutted path known as Prestolee Road is the way to the top length. At the top of this very steep path a turn to the right led to a small wooden bridge over which was the canal towing path in the direction of Bury. I had travelled this way only once before so there was a lot to see, and all of interest, but even so it seemed a long way from the top of the locks to the turn from which the headgear of the colliery could be seen. It was not with any feeling of enthusiasm that I made the approach, but rather with the thought, "Well, it's something fresh." I drew closer to the place where I was to work for many years, and to the experience which was to give me the ambition and determination from which I have had so much.

Anyone walking along the towing path the way I had come could be seen at some distance by the people at the colliery, and so

39

it was that "mi dad" was waiting for me. From the far side of the canal he pushed across an empty boat: "Get in, I'll pull you over," and as I gingerly stepped from the coping on to the little standing board in the boat I noticed a lot of water swilling about in the bottom. I remember thinking, "I wonder if it's going to sink," but the far side was gained without mishap and I was helped ashore. "So you found us all right?" "Yes. It's a long way, isn't it?" "It is. See anybody you knew?" "No", and with that very enlightening conversation we moved to the boat dock where a boat was taking shape on the stocks. To make conversation, "mi dad" said, "Number 68. All our boats have numbers rather than names." He then showed me as much as he could of the immediate surroundings, and this he did with the pride and enthusiasm always noticeable in anything to do with his work.

The dock was well roofed and enclosed on three sides against the elements. It had a wooden floor and it was, as I found out later, a comfortable place to work, light and airy. "Here's the cabin." We entered a spacious stone building at the west end of the dock. "We keep our tools and anything else of value in here." I looked round, noticing the tool boxes and racks of tools, the long work bench which stretched the length of one wall under two large windows, the saw benches and boxes of bolts and nails, but the massive iron fireplace with the large oven took my eye most of all. Even though it was August and a warm day at that, there was a roaring fire in that grate, and all the years I was to know it that fire was never out. "That's where we warm our dinners," I was told, and in the years that followed I certainly warmed some dinners and enjoyed them. If working "on t'cut" did anything for me it was to lay the foundation of a very healthy appetite along with a liking for good food. People often marvelled at the large amount which got packed into my small frame; I was by no means a strapping lad at 14 years of age but it was often said, "Ee cud eyt uh 'orse un then look fer t'tharniss!"

The initial inspection of the place over, my father suggested that we should go to see "Young Bill". This was Mr William Hayward, the manager, who was generally referred to (not to his face) in this way because his father, the former manager and then Agent, was known as "Owd John". The Hayward family had been at Ladyshore almost as long as my own, there was a close affinity between the families and to each Ladyshore was more than a place of employment. The Fletchers, the owners, were more to us than bosses; this was the situation when I started at Ladyshore and when it ceased, because of legislation, I left the same day.

We met Mr Hayward, a rather quiet man with a dry sense of humour, rarely given to smiling, and the first impression was rather off-putting. "So this is him, eh Rafe?" "Yes, Mr Hayward." "Right, then. Do as your dad tells you and you will be all right; he's certainly my best man." Little did I then realise how much truth there was in the words Young Bill had just spoken – it took many years for me to appreciate the real worth of "mi dad" to the Company.

The following morning at seven o'clock I started work in the boat dock with rather mixed feelings, and those mixed feelings continued until the day I left for good, too many years later.

The boat dock gang consisted of "mi dad" as foreman, two tradesmen, two general labourers and an old man who made and repaired the "boxes", or containers with which the boats were fitted. Then there was myself, apprentice or general dogsbody. They were a likable lot, with the exception of one of the tradesmen, whom I disliked at once; a dislike which was to develop into detestation. The first few days were more than interesting; everything was new and to a lad absolutely fascinating. My father gave me a tool box and my grandfather (mi dad's dad) gave me all his tools – a splendid and comprehensive collection. (I still have them and use them with pleasure.) These received much attention; I polished and learned to sharpen them and I was more than eager to learn how to use them with proficiency, but that took some time.

The first day I entered the cabin I was able to look at the many strange and what at that time seemed to be wonderful things. The most fascinating were on a low shelf to the right of the fireplace – four enormous steel hooks, the largest I have ever seen, almost six feet in length and three inches in diameter. Each had a thread for half its length and each was fitted with a nut of appropriate size. There were also four large square plates or washers, alongside which was a hook,

Boat Dock, Ladyshore

(Drawing by Peter Mills)

41

much smaller both in length and diameter, fitted with a large butterfly nut and again a large square plate. All these were in perfect condition, well oiled, free from dust or rust and I stood for some time looking at these marvels. Being of an inquisitive nature I eventually asked what they were, to which the reply was, "We use them for getting up sunken boats." I chewed this over for some time and could not come up with a reasonable idea as to how some well oiled screws could lift a sunken boat, nor did I at that time think that the coils of clean, heavy chain which reposed on a nearby shelf were used in such salvage operations.

The hooks had a rather hypnotic attraction for me. Every time I went into the cabin I was drawn towards them and every time I looked up my eyes went in the direction of their shelf. I found myself wishing a boat to sink and often when I touched them I got an imaginary tingle of electricity from them. I could hardly wait for an opportunity in which the magic of the screws would be demonstrated.

As general dogsbody my first duty in the morning was to see that the big iron kettle was filled, put on the fire so that there was the usual brew for everyone and then filled again so as to be available as a gesture of hospitality to the many people who made it their business to "call in t'dock" and to fill their cans. Over a short period of time I had made this duty into a form of ritual, with one or two calling places in the course of my work - a word with the blacksmiths, "Hello" to the firehole chaps and a "Good morning" to the winder in the big engine house. It was all very wrong and against regulations, but then...

One morning, after the normal routine, I was strolling back to the cabin as though tomorrow would do and I had just entered the dock when an unusual state of activity caught my attention. At that same moment a voice very close to my ear asked, with a studied politeness which could have been heard several miles away, "Weerst bin? Ee's bin axin' fer thi. They'll git bloody scalped one o' these days, just thee see when ee gets 'is ons on thi. Oouh? Oouh? You lickle bugger, ah'd u good mind t'do it misel! Git thi bloody skates on!" After such words of welcome the labourer, who from my very first day at Ladyshore had been my friend (and sometimes protector) spoke that magic phrase which set my blood racing. "Wi' get'n one deyn ut Bury." "No!" "Yay, wi'an." With that assurance I sped down the dock into the cabin, put the kettle on the hob, turned and gave a hand with lifting the screws from their resting place. Several labourers from other parts of the colliery workshops had augmented our own small gang (as always at such times as these), a motor wagon had backed up to the far end of the dock and already assembled equipment was being loaded. My father was not to be seen just then and I was at a loss as to what to do next. So I asked the nearest person to me. "Use thi'yed," was the grunted answer, and a second glance confirmed the speaker's identity. Another voice, more kindly: "Thet none fer tut lad," and then to me, "Aw them scopes as is in t'lawft, un then brew fer us all. After thes done that come un gimme a lift." So off I went again and in no time at all I was back helping to load the waggon. Mi dad was there. "Have you made tea for everybody?" I was asked. "Yes." "Right lads, we'll get a drink and a bite to eat and then we must be off." With that we all moved to the cabin, tea was shared with the extra men and a sandwich or a bit of cake offered and taken. "There weren't bi no chance uh nowt ut Bury," remarked one of the older hands. "Yon mon'll not be pleased ut us gooin', yon mon i't'office." "Oh, why?" asked the greenhorn (me). "Ee doesn't like us. Ee doesn't like nobody, they'll see fer thi'sel," and then the voice of authority called, "Come on, lads, let's be having yer." Out we all trooped, picking up working coats on the way, prompted again by those with experience, and got into the open back of the waggon. I was haunching down by the tailgate when, "Not theer, lad. 'Ere wi me – warmer an' no wind." "Thanks." Just as I was settling down to be as comfortable as possible, my father looked over the side as he was getting into the cab with the driver. "Took some time with that kettle earlier on." He said no more but his face had the expression of thunder. "Ee's get'n it on 'im, as Little Rafe, so watch it," was the advice whispered in my ear. The lorry with its "load of equipment and sin" as some wag said, was on its way to Bury Wharf and for me a new adventure.

The speed of the vehicle whipped up particles of coal dust, residue of a previous loaded journey, stinging faces, ears and necks. The biting November wind did nothing to help; the metal-sheathed side-boards offered nothing in the way of cushioning and the waggon bottom was wet and slippery. I made my usual effort at conversation: "I've never been to Bury." "Thet gooin' ney," came the muffled reply. "What's it like?" "Wot's wot like?" "Bury." "It's er, it's er, it's like Bury. Stop bein' uh grammerschool lad, axin' nowt but questions. Shut thi'ole." We had a wonderful understanding, my friend and I. It looked as though people might be the least bit on edge and tempers perhaps on the frayed side, but despite the discomfort of the journey we seemed to arrive all too soon at Bury Wharf. The unloading started at once, watched from the office doorway by a small, sour-faced man. My father nodded a greeting in his direction, but with no response.

The waggon was unloaded on the cold, draughty wharf without the slightest hitch and everything was handled with care and placed in orderly lines or lots. The experts said that nothing had been forgotten, and the screws, when their turn came, were handled with even greater care. "Steady wi' them. Ee thinks they're made o'gowld, does Little Rafe." The sarcasm, the taut nerves – I was at a loss with such unusual behaviour.

Whilst the unloading and sorting had been in progress my
father had gone in search of the offending vessel and I could
now see him returning. As he came nearer he said, "It's on the
outside at Number Three. They've moved the inside boat and
I've picked out a pair of empties." After a slight pause he
added, "It's starting to rain," and I then noticed that
raindrops were spattering the surface of the canal.

The two empty boats were immediately loaded with such
equipment as would be needed and then they were handled to
the place where the sunken boat lay. "It's Trencherbone," mi
dad said in answer to a question about the cargo. (Evidently
a cargo of Trencherbone was preferable to a cargo of nuts or
slack in a sunken boat; being a larger section coal it did not
hold the water like the other two and so the job was easier, or
so the experts said.) The empties, or camels, as we shall now
call them (this being a salvage job) were placed one on each
side of the casualty. All I could see was an open stretch of
rainswept water as I stood by mi dad's side. "It's eight or
nine inches under," he said, when he noticed my puzzled look.
The camels in position, baulks of pitchpine, 6" by 6" and about
20 feet in length, were placed athwart the camels and over the
shoulders of the sunken boat. A long line, the ends of which
were held by men on the camels, was lowered as a part loop
and guided by a boathook down the outside of the stem post of
the sunken boat to the bed of the cut. The men on the camels
began pulling and easing their respective ends in a sawing
effect, the idea being to work the line under the submerged
vessel. However, after only a few minutes it was obvious that
the object was not to be achieved in this way; the sunken boat
was lying on a hard bottom.

The camels were eased for'd a little and as if by some
conjuring trick the single screw with the butterfly nut
appeared and was placed in position on the baulks. The large
flat plate on which the nut turned rested on top of the timbers,
and the hook hung down as near as makes no difference over
the stem post. A man wearing knee-length rubber boots gingerly
lowered himself on to the unseen deck and the short chain which
he held in his hand was threaded through the ring bolt on the
stem plate. Would it hold? It was to be hoped so. Men were
already at the large wing nut; oil had been squirted on to the
steel plate, turning the nut tightened the chain, and as this
continued with care the bows of the camels dipped ever so
slightly. Still the nut was turned. "Easy now. Take it steady."
There was a disturbance of water, as though a large bubble
was coming to the surface and the shape of the sunken deck
could be seen. "Hold it there. Try yer lines again." This time
way was made and the lines were judged to be under the
shoulder of the sunken boat. The heavy chains were then tied
to one end of the line and steadily lowered into the water
whilst the team on the other end hauled away. Up came the

soggy, slutchy rope and the dirty liquid dripped off hands – that which did not run down arms to soak coat sleeves. Up came the end of the chain; another pull or two and then, "That's it." Both ends were for the moment made fast and the position of the camels adjusted. "Now let's get stern end done." Attention was now transferred to the opposite end of the casualty and the small hook and so on were all moved aft.

The for'd end was not left altogether, and several men moved the baulks into place and positioned the big hooks ready for the lift. A small, rather unsteady platform or walkway of planks was arranged so that the massive spanners could be worked. Once again the main effort was astern, but there seemed to be a problem – the rudder of the submerged craft was hampering progress (but I can not recall such a phrase being used!) and short ropes and a couple of boathooks were applied with difficulty in a very restricted space without avail. There was a lot of huffing and puffing, and "What th'ell dust think thet doin'?" was asked of one person who forgot he was not wearing wellingtons as he stepped on to the submerged sternplate in enthusiasm. Suddenly out slid the large iron rudder pin and then the rudder. The way was now clear to try the line under the stern and this time the ropes slid easily and the chain was soon under the shoulder. In no time at all the lifting gear was ready and the second rickety platform was in place. The rain was by now falling steadily, making already precarious footholds more so.

Four teams, two men to each screw, two screws at each end, commenced the lift. One man pulled and one pushed on each of the large ring spanners which tightened the nuts on the screws, walking in a tight circle over the rickety improvised walkways. From the first step the tension on the chains was noticeable and so was the settlement of the camels. The water between them became disturbed then, as though it was boiling, and first the stem and then the small deck of the submerged vessel appeared above the surface. It was not easy; the lifting teams were changed several times. It was a case of "Come on, lad" and I pushed and strained at the big key, round and round, round and round on the uncertain foothold. The spell seemed endless but in fact it was of very short duration and it was with thanks that I heard, "Let me have it" and a helping hand steadied me as I let go the spanner. I thankfully straightened my back and as I came upright such a giddy sensation took hold – if a pair of strong hands had not held me for a second or so I would most certainly have gone "in t'cut". "Thanks," I muttered through chattering teeth, for I now realised it was raining as though there was a cloudburst and I was sweating and frozen at the same time. As the giddy spell passed one of the scoops was pushed at me; the gunnels were just above the water and this was quite enough, so I was told. "Find a place and get crackin'," I heard in my ear. "We must set an example – start first and finish last." I nodded, nipped smartly on to

45

the wet deck of the boat and set to work as though there was
no tomorrow. The scoop, a large bucket-type, three gallon
capacity, was attached to a shaft about four feet long and was
not the easiest thing to handle, especially when bent almost
double. It was a backbreaking task, but everyone worked like
demons, arms going like pistons in an effort to ladle the water
from the boat to the canal. My shoulders were as though split,
my arms ready to drop off, and as from a far distance I heard
Tommy, who was next to me: "Do thi gud. They'll 'ave muscles
after - some uz they should 'ave and some uz they shouldn't."
I made no reply. I was sweating, wet through, water was
coming out of my laceholes and we were all the same. It must
have been turned one o'clock and a jug of tea would have been
appreciated. After another half hour of the same graft, I
decided. Nipping smartly off the now floating but still waterlogged boat, across the inside camel to the banking, I walked
towards the group of buildings which were Ladyshore Depot. At
the office door but standing back out of the rain was the clerk
and through the open door I could see a cheerful fire with a
kettle on the hob. "Excuse me, sir, is it possible to have a
brew? We don't have a can with us," I said in my most charming
and polite manner. His sour face clouded, it became flushed,
and a choking voice replied, "'Ave a brew? No!" I realised how
Oliver Twist must have felt. "Get off my office step now, or I
will report you to Mr Hayward and get your time docked." I
was stunned. Never before had I been treated in this manner.
I came of a respectable family, my father held a position of
responsibility, my people had been part of the Company since
it was first formed. I must admit that I was in a rather
bedraggled state and I would not have got past the
commissionaire at the Savoy, but damn it all, I only wanted a
brew. "Ah said get," Sour-face said, and almost in tears of
rage I turned on my heel and went back to my allotted post.

My short journey had not gone unnoticed and when I got back
my father asked kindly, "Well, did you get what you went for?"
I was unable to answer, I was too full. "If we put our backs
into it we can have a hot drink when we get back." So with
that I scrambled to where I had been before the incident and
temper coupled with the determination for revenge made my arms
work like pistons. I forgot that I was wet, uncomfortable, dirty
and thirsty .- my one thought was that I had been insulted, for
no reason, and through me my father and a gang of very good
men. I must have realised then that I did not have my father's
even temperament and I was certain that nobody would   treat
me in such a manner with impunity.

The light faded early on this cold, wet winter's day; it was
dusk before we had the boat dry and it was totally dark by the
time it had been moved to a position under the crane so that
it could be unloaded. I stood watching the four hooks being
attached to the first box and heard the chuffing of the steam

engine as the container was lifted easily out of the loaded boat. I felt rather than saw a movement close at hand and a stooping figure emerged from the gloom. A voice like gravel said, "Bin a bad day fer yo lot." Turning, I saw a gangling, rough-looking man, standing at his ease like a broken prop, bent slightly forward from the waist, thumbs in his belt. "It certainly has," I replied. "They looks fed up," he said. "I am." "Ast 'ad no meyt?" "No." "Ner nowt sup?" "None of us have since we left Ladyshore." After a pause he turned and quietly disappeared.

The mills and warehouses which formed the wharf complex at Bury were ablaze with light. Gas lamps had been lit in the coal wharf office, it was just after four o'clock by the wallclock there, and I noticed that my father was standing at the open doorway to the office, speaking to somebody. I went over to him. "I've asked him to ring for transport." All the gear used in the operation of the day was in the process of assembly for the return journey and as soon as the motor arrived loading began at once. The boat which had been sunk was by now unloaded and placed in a safe berth against the morning and I was doing what I could to help when again ·I heard the gravel voice: "'Ere, get raynd this 'ere," and a can of hot, steaming tea was pushed into my hand. "Bout milk, wi a'none," and he then went to distribute several similar cans to the others of our people. I filled the can lid and then took the

Canal at Elton c1910

(F Sunderland)

47

remainder of the tea to my dad. He must have been as wet, tired, cold and miserable as any of us, but such was his nature that he would rather have died than betray such weakness. He was still brisk and straight-backed and his stocky figure radiated his authority. I gave him the can of tea, from which he drank gratefully and then immediately looked for another person to whom he could pass it on. I told him of the man whose kindness was the source of that welcome drink. "That'll be Joe Lansdale; he's the charge hand on the puddle boat, a Company boat." I collected the now empty cans and took them along to our friend. "Thank you so much, Mr Lansdale; these cans were greatly appreciated." I got a funny look. "Cons were clen - ah swilled um i't'cut afore ah brewed i' Cromp'ns fire 'ole." "Thanks again," I said and moved off. As the years rolled on I was to see a lot of Joe. We were never friends; it was not his nature to have a friend, but I liked him and perhaps in his own funny way he liked me - but anyway we had respect for each other.

The loading of the gear was completed in double-quick time, everything was aboard the lorry and nothing left, then all the gang climbed on board. It was not as uncomfortable as it had been on the outward journey. The metal sides had rather a cushioned feel and the bottom, although swimming in water, was not as slippery as it had been earlier. However, I was thankful to find a corner out of the wind and rain. What the hell! I could not get any wetter or more dirty than I was, and nothing mattered any more.

"Art gooin' eyt t'neet?" asked my friend. "Yes," I replied. "They's sin Bury un they's sin one gett'n up so wot dust 'ave t'say?" I did not answer, thinking to shut him up, but I was wrong. He tried again, "That shut thi up fer once. Lickle Rafe were reet pleased wi' thi - ah axt 'im un ee sed ee were." I muttered a thank you, and perhaps it sounded rather ungrateful. "Dit not yar mi? Ah sed art gooin' eyt t'neet?" "Yes, to nightschool." "Neetskoo? Neetskoo? Wot dust want do that fer?" "I'm taking a commercial course." Silence. This time I had achieved the knock-out.

The return journey did not take as long as the outward one and in a relatively short time our transport was backing up to the boat dock. As it stopped I gathered an armful of ropes, wedges and a maul and ran as best I could in the dark along the dock. On reaching the cabin I fumbled for the light switch, found it and on came the glims which served to illuminate the dock area. The cabin was warm, the fire was still good and the kettle, almost full, was near to boiling. Grabbing the two largest jugs I put in some tea and then running back to the lorry I gave a hand once again with the unloading. Two or three minutes later, again loaded with tools, I was scampering towards the cabin. The two jugs were filled from the kettle, tea was made and off back to the lorry. I helped with lifting and carrying to and fro until all the gear was stowed away and the big screws were on the cabin floor, drying so that they could be cleaned and oiled and carefully put in their place in the morning.

"Ee's a good un, is this lad," greeted the handing out of the freshly brewed tea. Wet coats and overalls were placed so that the warm atmosphere of the cabin would have them dry by morning. I put on my bike clips; my trousers were soaking wet, I did not have a dry pair, but I did have a warm dry coat and gloves as well as a waterproof hat, all new only a week or so ago. I wheeled out my bike and waited for my dad, then we made our way through the pit yard. I punched the time clock - it was almost six o'clock, my first bit of overtime and I remember feeling rather "chuffed". The rain was still bucketing, shining like steel stair rods in the powerful beams from our carbide lamps. "Are you tired?" Dad asked. "I am," I replied. Then after a pause I said, "Are they always like that to us at Bury Wharf?" "Yes, at least he is." "Can you not do anything about it?" After a minute, "I could, but it's not worth the bother. Don't let it worry you. These things are all part of growing up." I had heard that phrase before and would again many times, and even now, fifty years later, it comes to mind on occasions.

That day of the sunken boat was the first time I had seen and taken part in the use of those large hooks, and as so often happens, in using them their fascination was gone. I had seen and taken part in the raising of a sunken boat, not an experience often repeated in the years which were to follow, years which made but little change in the methods employed. The only difference was perhaps the replacement of the scoops by portable hand-operated suction pumps (a cutting down on the britches arse steam), but the remainder of the work was the same; the camels and lifting gear (those magnificent hooks and chains) remained unchanged.

During the years which followed I worked in one capacity or another at Bury Wharf; the second time was about two years later. The office building had been forcibly entered with some resultant damage; I had gone up to the office at Ladyshore for something or other and was seen by Mr Hayward (Young Bill), who spoke of the incident. He said, "Go and see what you can do; a new lock, see to the door and window, whatever it needs. Take your mate with you. Tom will take you when he comes back. I'll let your father know as soon as I see him; no doubt you will be there a day or two." (Dad had gone to Farnworth Bridge a short time earlier.)

Tools were hastily gathered and in an hour we had been dropped at Bury Wharf. The reception accorded was far from welcoming and in no uncertain manner I was told, "Think on, no messin'. Ahm none avin' im in mi office. They'll be bad enough," and this was whilst I was on the doorstep. I did not take kindly to such treatment and to say that I was astounded would be an understatement. My training, at home and in my activities away from work, was on the basis that loyalty must be acknowledged by reciprocation and that those who were privileged to command should in their turn show loyalty to the men in their charge.

Tommy was and always had been my loyal friend and in a way he was in my charge. My reaction and reply were no doubt prompted and perhaps stimulated by the pent-up fury of two years' standing. Two years in which my vocabulary had been considerably enlarged and I had learned that there were those people who understood a remonstrance only if it were couched in the most forceful terms. It was with a feeling of revulsion that I verbally dressed him down, at the end of which the wide-eyed, gaping tally clerk gasped, "Ahl tell Mesther 'Ayward abayt this." "No doubt you will; it is your privilege. Your telephone is there." With no more ado I strode into the office to get on with the job according to the instructions I had been given. Grinning like the proverbial cat, Tommy followed with my bag of tools and during the next two days our comings and goings and necessary work went unremarked.

In due course Mr Hayward, the Colliery Manager, gave my father the version of the incident which he himself had been given; the old man was rather troubled and doubtless his face showed it, and then Young Bill remarked, "Not quite the young gentleman we thought, eh?" This was said with a wry smile, which was quickly noticed, and with a relieved chuckle the reply was, "No, I never thought he was angelic." There the matter ended officially.

A few days later, after tea, I was on the receiving end of a very strong homily, the theme of which was respect for my elders, topped off with the admonition to "watch my language".

Cleaning the Harbour

Loading coal into boats at the several collieries along the canal necessitated dredging of the loading areas at frequent intervals as the coal had a disgusting habit at times of missing the boat and falling into the cut.

Several collieries had loading points off the main canal and Ladyshore was one such, having a harbour loading facility under the screening plant. The coal was processed, dirt, stone and other foreign bodies were removed by hand, then the coal was segregated into various lump sizes by a variety of grids. Each of the grades passed by chutes to conveyor belts which in turn deposited each particular type into the boat for which it was intended; Trencherbone, slack or nuts. Ideally the boat should be positioned to receive the load; if the supervisor was

50

a diligent man there was no problem and the loss was minimal, but human nature being what it is, often the conveyor belt and the boat were not in harmony, therefore an annual running off and cleaning of the harbour was necessary. This work could only be done at weekend and then only if the pits were not working on the Saturday morning. It will be realised that some planning was involved.

First, notice had to be given to the Canal Company of the intention, and permission obtained to drain off the water. All the gear to be used had to be checked, repaired or replaced as need be.

On the appointed Friday, at the end of the working day, all the boats were moved from the harbour and a gang of men prepared to run off the water. At intervals the canal bankings come together as a bottle neck, and at such places both bankings are for some distance stone built. At the narrowest point a channel has been cut in the stonework from the coping downwards, and this extends below the waterline to a stone sill which crosses the bed of the canal to the base of a similar cutting in the opposite stone-reinforced banking. At these stockgates, as they are called, on the far banking, are a number of stout planks of timber, about nine inches by five inches, slightly tapered at each end and four large iron handles, one on each side at each end. The purpose of all this is to enable the canal to be closed off so that lengths can be drained when necessary.

There were stockgates just inside the entrance to the harbour and also a pile of planks, and this was the scene of the initial activity. A plank was put across the narrow neck and, with a long pole, a scraper on the end, the stone sill was cleared of mud, old boots, parts of old bikes and any other rubbish accumulated in twelve months. It was not an easy task to walk the plank and manipulate the scraper at the same time and the job took about half an hour to do. Whilst this was in progress other hands were unchaining the dam planks (some said damn!) and putting them in order close to the bank. Each plank was numbered in order of usage (the numbers were cut into the planks) and a stiff brush was vigorously applied, making sure that all were clean and in good order.

By then the man walking the plank (always providing that a mishap had not occurred) should have had the sill clear of obstructions, and all was ready for the cutting-off. The dam planks were by no means lightweight and even though a second plank had been put across the water it was not easy to manhandle them into their places, with the flats of the faces towards the water and the bevelled ends inward; it was work for hefty lads. With the planking in place, each one weighing the previous one down, there was then the vital job of securing the dam and making it watertight. Weight was put on the top

Gang working on the canal between Nob End and Bailey Bridge. Front left: Sam Rigg. Centre left: John Lansdale. Centre Right: Joe Lansdale. (AW)

plank whilst the ends were firmly wedged, and this job sorted the men from the boys. The entire gang were required to stand on the top plank - imagine balancing on a five-inch-wide bit of wood less than six inches above the water with a large expanse in front and the Lord knows how much wet at the back of you; not only balancing but shuffling to make room for the next man and then standing still for several minutes so that the wedges could be driven down the stone channel. Sometimes there was a cry and a splash and, "Ah corn't swim!" "Ney's thi chance fer t'larn!" The more fortunate would get ashore by walking the plank with dry feet and give assistance to the two who were flapping about in the water. They would be hauled to dry land with: "'Ast no moor sense ut thy age?" to be told, "**** ***". The two unfortunates would shamble off home having taken an early bath; at that time pit head baths were a long way in the future. Such incidents had their funny side, and very often, knowing the persons involved, the words of the song came to mind:-

> They had water so it appeared,
> Where water never had been for years,
> At the back of the neck and behind the ears,
> Said Slippery Sam the Stoker.

The planks in place and wedged, the sluice paddle over the drainage culvert was lifted fractionally, allowing a controlled flow of water into the passage which led down the hillside to a short distance above river level. A man stationed down the ravine noted the outflow and in due course he signalled to the person detailed to keep him under observation that the tunnel was clear and all seemed to be well. The sluice was then lifted higher and the outflow increased, but the two men on watch remained at their posts until the harbour was drained, a tedious job but necessary.

There was then a time of waiting; pipes and fags were lit and everybody leisurely watched the water level. It was some time before any noticeable fall was seen; the sluice was then opened further and the fall became faster; meanwhile the dam was under careful attention, any squirts of water being stopped by running a spadeful of very fine pepper coal dust along the seam joint of the plank on the pressure side (the side open to the canal).

After a couple of hours the water level was very much lower in the harbour and islands could be seen under the screens. The squirts in the dam had stopped, the sluice paddle was fully open, and in another quarter of an hour the bottom was bare. It was then decided to leave the job for the night and a watchman had been detailed in the course of planning to watch the site until morning. Not that it was feared that anything untoward would happen, but no chances were taken. After a last look round and the calling in of the watchers on the ravine, it was "Right lads" and off trooped the gang.

On Saturday, six o'clock start, the gang (very appreciative of the extra money these maintenance jobs provided) were eager to get on with it. The harbour bottom had the look of a lunar landscape – piles of dust here, Trencherbone there, slack, nuts and burgee interspersed with shallow pools of dirty water; the whole a soggy, drab grey.

In a spurt of enthusiasm several people jumped down into the harbour, others handed down planks of wood and a wheelbarrow thudded into the mess. "Ney then, ney then, let's have some order! Percy, get these lads of thine organised in a proper manner," came the voice of authority, as my father noticed the possibility of chaos. Under his critical eye, iron plates were laid on the banking, planking platforms and runways formed a pattern on the bottom, a further two or three barrows were carefully handed down and groups of men took up positions at the several hillocks of coal. The backbreaking work of harbour cleaning began in earnest. The spaders filled the barrows, the wheelers trundled along the planking to one of several sets of plates by the harbour wall, tipped and returned. The tipped coal was then thrown spadeful by spadeful up on to the plates on the banking and in turn spaded into coal tubs (small waggons). When these were full they were pushed along a roughly laid railtrack and left for screening on the following Monday.

For the first hour or two the work went along as normal, with the usual interchange of spaders and wheelers and with the tradesmen lending a hand to "spell" the labour.

Half past eight – breakfast time and a very welcome half hour break. Those who have ever done demanding work of this nature will understand the appreciation of a can of tea, a bite to eat and a leisurely smoke (not that on jobs of this kind smoking was banned, in fact cigarettes and pipes were on the go all the time, but that is not the same as a smoke taken comfortably).

Canal water, it would seem, has a rather cementing effect on some types of coal, particularly dust and slack, and work on the accumulations of these two took longer than on those of the larger-section coal. Gradually the piles disappeared and then it was the time for careful supervision. The puddle lining of the harbour must not be damaged; if it were the results would be devastating and in this particular instance the mine shaft so close to the waterway could be irreparably damaged, or the banking might burst and be washed down into the river far below. The men for the most part were aware of these dangers and consequently careful, but the responsibility was mi dad's. Such was his nature that this was never delegated or shirked. He might have been a dozen men, he was in so many places at once: "Good, no more here." "That's enough." "A nice job, lads." After he was satisfied, and only then, he gave the order for the harbour to be cleared and then he inspected the sill and seating of the sluice paddle. With everything in order and in its place, the paddle firmly home, it was time for the final stages.

Clearing the equipment from the harbour was not done in record time; the early morning enthusiasm had evaporated rather. Arms and backs were sore, hands were bruised and there was a general feeling of fatigue. It was rather well put by one lad: "Ahm bloody done!"

By this time the cleaned harbour was giving off a rather pungent smell, and so were the men who had worked in it. They were particularly glad to see the last of the planks and plates deposited on the banking and Percy had his men disperse them in no time at all.

Now was the testing time – the rewatering of the harbour. At this point I was aware of the arrival of a person who was not one of our lot. He was the Deputy Superintendent of the Canal, an officer of the Canal Company who had come along to see that the rewatering was to his employers' requirements.

Again men descended the steep ravine to keep a watch on the culvert. The lookout was posted on the rim and with a final look at the sluice paddle the wedges on the dam planks were eased off and water began to run into the empty loading area. It was very controlled and under watchful eyes. Soon the planks were lifted one by one as the unhurried job proceeded, the men down the ravine signalled that there was no problem at their end and all the time the water was running in at a controlled rate. The equipment was collected ready for its return to its normal resting place, but the gang was not yet dispersed.

After more than an hour the large empty area of not so long ago was looking almost normal. There was very little flow from the main canal and the exercise was almost over, apart from one last inspection, the pit shaft.

My father and one man went off to the pit head, clambered on to the cage and at a signal to the winder the cage, with them on top of it, was very slowly lowered down the shaft so that they could inspect the stone and brick lining for any unusual signs of water seepage. After about half an hour they had returned to the top satisfied, the equipment was cleared away, the gang dispersed, the lookouts and those men in the ravine called in and we made our way back to the cabin to clean up (to get rid of the stink!) and to have the final brew of the day. In this we were joined by the Company man: "Thanks, lad; allus a good brew 'ere!" The harbour cleaning was over for another year.

The very line of the Manchester, Bolton and Bury Canal, the fact that it followed the rims of the valleys of two rivers for the major part of its length, demanded the highest standard of maintenance and a constant awareness of the state of the embankments and buttressing (both natural and man-made). These very often gave the impression of being little more than an eggshell in thickness, with an almost sheer drop of 80-90 feet to the river below.

The Canal Company were responsible for the maintenance and general wellbeing of the waterway, isolated instances such as the harbour cleaning excepted, and for this purpose there were two depots, one at Oldfield Road, Salford, and the main one at Nob End, Little Lever. In addition, there was a smaller and infrequently used one at Giant's Seat, just south of Ringley.

Nob End was ideally located for a main depot. Strategically placed on the Bolton to Bury length at the head of the staircase of locks which descended to the Manchester length, it was spacious, with plenty of storage room for large stocks of undressed stone. There was a roomy, if windswept, stonemasons' yard, a very useful smithy and an extensive carpenters' shop. Nob End had all of these, plus the facilities to repair and if necessary to build canal boats and flats, with adequate

Launching the Puddling Boat at Nob End   *(D Stones)*

moorings for their fleet should it ever be in the home port at the same time.

The depots were established whilst the canal was in building, with the same families providing the workforce over the years, or near enough. The Superintendent and his deputy were both stonemasons, this trade being considered (by the Canal Company) as far superior to any other. The pay was higher and being a stonemason for the Company was a job much sought after and envied. The stone gang (which included bricklayers and labourers) had as transport the flagship of the Company fleet, *Stonemasons' Flat*, a vessel twice the width of the ordinary narrow boat, decked and with a large hold, and on deck was a derrick for lifting, the usual array of tools and ladders, and a for'd locker for bags of cement. There was a well-appointed, spacious cabin aft and the craft was in spotless condition, so clean that it gave the impression that its deck had been "holystoned". The lines and tackle were also shipshape and those who manned the vessel were of smart and clean appearance. This was the general tone of the Company men — clean and efficient, no scruff.

Boatbuilders and carpenters formed the second largest gang, and as they had to make and repair the massive lock gates the workshop facilities were in proportion and the "hard" was large enough to take the flat as and when necessary. The standard of craftsmanship was high, their working areas always tidy.

A smithy was also important to the canal and its wellbeing. Apart from constantly making and repairing ironwork, the smith kept the large variety of tools in good working order and provided the expertise to make the one-off as and when the need arose. The Nob End Depot had a good smithy.

The labouring gangs manned the cut maintenance boats, the puddle gang kept the canal bed in order as well as attending to minor repairs to the banking and the dredger gang removed the old bedsteads, bikes, dustbins, buckets, pans and so on which the "out of sight, out of mind" morons dumped. Very often the boat had the appearance of a floating rag and bone cart. This job was vital to the smooth operation of the canal system.

These boats and several other narrow boats each had a cabin complete with the traditional iron stove with its tin chimney, used for eating and storage purposes and, most important, protection in rainy weather. It was only on very, very rare occasions that Company boats worked in the rain or snow.

One of the duties of the gangers was to inspect daily the length in which their boat was working. The superintendent and his deputy walked the entire lengths at least twice in the week for the purpose of inspection, and on Sunday morning every week all the men on the depot, tradesmen, gangers and labourers alike, each inspected an allocated section, its banking and supports for traces of faults. For this they all received extra pay and no doubt it was well appreciated. They did the chore diligently, but even so, many times the banking collapsed with considerable damage and over the lifetime of the canal caused a heavy financial drainage, so much so that in the 1820's the Company wanted to close the entire system and build a railway. This move was strongly opposed by the coal interests; the coal merchants in particular. Parliamentary ruling was that a railway could be built from Bolton to Manchester, but the canal must be kept open and well maintained so long as required. It remained fully operational until the final devastating banking collapse on the Little Lever side of Nob End in 1936. After that the canal was workable from Bailey Bridge to Bury and was used by Ladyshore Coal Company until it was closed by the Coal Board in 1951.

The Ice Boat

For a youth to start work or change occupation is a fascinating experience. Each day presents a fresh adventure and that was how the years I spent on the canal started.

It was generally accepted that I was normal, although there were those people who doubted it; it would be very pretentious of me to claim a thirst for knowledge and most likely the description so often used, "nosey little sod" was very near the mark. But there was so much to be seen and so many things to be done and be part of. Mealtimes round the cabin fire often stimulated discussion amongst my elders (and, I was never allowed to forget, my betters). Often such discussions encouraged rather than dampened my enthusiasm.

It was very near the beginning of my boatbuilding years on one such dinner time, when the warm August and fine September had given way to autumn and that in its turn to an early winter, that reference was made to "th'ice boat" and someone said, "Wi'st 'at bi gerrin' it up."

Eating was usually my most pleasurable recreation but now I sat rigidly, a sandwich halfway to my face, mouth open, eyes no doubt as big as saucers and ears flapping. I was afraid to miss a single word. "We'll have a look after dinner." My ability to put away considerable quantities of food at remarkable speed had often surprised people, but on this occasion all my previous records were broken and I waited impatiently for the end of dinner time, looking all the time expectantly at mi dad.

"Come on then. You're like a cat on hot bricks," he said, and together we walked out of the cabin. At least, he walked. "Steady on. It'll not run away," came from behind me, so obediently, if reluctantly, I followed (literally) in my father's footsteps; he knew where he was going, I didn't.

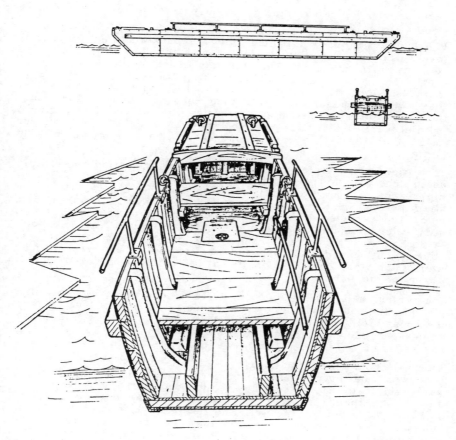

Th'Ice Boat   *(Drawing by Brian Worthington)*

Outside the cabin we had turned right, down t'clough, as the length was called, along past the many loaded boats moored two abreast, and on still further almost to the "turnin' 'ole". Here we stopped and he looked down into the murky waters. At this point the banking was high, a good four feet above the water level, and all I could see was a spike which had been driven into the bank from which a rusty chain passed over the coping and down into the water. "Where is it?" "Here." "I can't see anything." "No, well it's on t'bottom. We always sink it in summer; keeps i'good fettle." I was very relieved; for one horrible moment I thought someone had pinched it, this boat with the magical-sounding name, a boat I had never even seen. "So now do we get it up?" I asked hopefully. "Perhaps next week." But more than a week passed before the exercise began.

I had by then been initiated into the backbreaking discomforts involved in raising a sunken boat and the Bury adventure was very fresh in my mind. But this was different; this was "th'ice boat". My mind boggled at the prospects and possibilities of journeys along the waterway to Radcliffe and on to Bury (at that time unfamiliar to me), along lengths which I knew only through conversations and anecdotes to which I had been privileged to listen. Life and working was a great adventure for me at that time; it always has been so and is now, in my late sixties.

The impedimenta relating to the salvage operation were duly assembled. On this exercise only one camel boat was used, the high banking serving that function on the inside. Only the small screws were required and the boat which appeared from below the surface was a surprise, different from anything I had seen before. It was shorter and narrower than a coal boat and it looked as though both ends had been broken off; it was oblong, butt-ended and each end was decked. There was an open well amidships, with handrails at a little over waist height along the gunnels.

The water had to be scooped out, so our arms worked like pistons and our shoulders soon ached. The water level inside the boat fell rapidly and at the same time the stagnant, unpleasant odour increased; it was a stink caused by the long immersion of oak timbers in water that was anything but clean.

After an hour of hard slogging (it felt more like a day) the boat was floating, though still waterlogged. In a short time it was possible to empty the bilge, which was not a very long job, and it was then I realised how responsive the boat was to the shifting of weight in the well and how easy it was to rock from side to side. My father explained that the boat when operational was steered by its crew putting their weight on one side or the other and that this buoyancy was the main feature of the Ladyshore Ice Boat, which had been the brainchild of my great-grandfather, a fine craftsman and a very practical man. Yet his employers had to comply with the then new coal mines regulations; because he was illiterate and unable to sign his name, Great-grandfather was superseded as General Manager of the Ladyshore Colliery Undertakings by a clerk. From this bitter blow the man never recovered and died of a broken heart.

Once the boat was raised and afloat, the next few days were ones of activity. A couple of labourers scraped, swilled and scrubbed and eventually the stagnant, pungent odour gave way to the normal boat smell and the Ice Boat was moved to its winter moorings, just in front of the boat dock cabin. The sheet iron plating was brushed down and given a good skin of tar; after buffing, several coats of red paint were applied to the handrails and where there was rust it was removed. After the balance had been adjusted it rode at its moorings a very smart craft, of which one was justly proud.

Not many years later, but under vastly different conditions, I was told, "Waiting is the worst part." It was certainly true in the early part of that winter – it was agony!

There were gales, rain, fog and sleet – anything but frost. Anxiously the afternoon sky was scanned for signs of a possible freeze; would it ever come? Was it going to be one of those unhealthy mild winters? Then, at long last, just a few days before Christmas, it was there, not a heavy frost but keen enough to put a skim of ice on the water. Ice is a danger to canal boats, particularly to those of timber construction, and it does not need to be thick. A mere skim of less than a quarter of an inch in thickness can cut through two-inch planking like a circular saw, or it can rip out the caulking from the seams. The Ice Boat with its armour-plated hull was a necessity in clearing a safe passage ahead of the normal traffic.

That morning, as soon as I got outside the house, the frost was sparkling on the ground, the bushes had a covering of hoar and this was it! Legs working overtime sped my bike along the way through Farnworth, down Peel Street, Wilson's Brow and over the Vat Waste. Excitedly I watched the road, in the powerful beam of my carbide lamp, come rushing towards me. I crossed

Nob End Locks

the little wooden bridge by the basin and then I had to push my bike up Nob Brow. It would not have been a surprise if my tyres had been steaming! At a half walk and half run, sobbing for breath, I struggled up the path by the side of the locks – were they frozen? I couldn't see. At the top and over the wooden footbridge on to the towing path, I directed the beam from my lamp on to the cut. Yes, there was ice – not a lot, not thick, but ice! The distance from there to Ladyshore on that morning was negligible, or so it seemed. Starting time was 7.00am and my eagerness had somehow shortened the journey so that I was clocking on at 6.45am. But I was not the first, the fire in the massive grate in the cabin was roaring away. "Ahm allus 'ere turnt six," came the answer to my unasked question. In no time at all I had filled the kettle, washed the jugs and had brewed tea by the time mi dad was propping his bike against his tool box.

"In a bit of a sweat this morning, lad," he said. "Yes," I replied. "Anything special?" "Well, there's frost and I thought you might let me..." "What?" The refusal in his voice was like a blow, my heart dropped into my boots and without even taking a drink of the tea I had made he went out to attend to his morning duties in the office.

I could feel myself red about the ears; perhaps tears were not very far away, but I had far too much pride for that. "Nay, lad," I thought, "we do not disgrace ourselves," and so with an empty feeling I began to get my tools together. As it was still dark outside I got a rudder post and after I had put it across a couple of benches began to dress it in a half-hearted fashion. There were all the pointers to a disappointing day. A couple of the labourers went out to see to the Ice Boat and the gear, other people went about their tasks; nobody spoke to me. I was thankful for that, I was far too miserable for any kind of chat. After a time I heard my father's quick footsteps coming along the dock and I sensed rather than saw him come into the cabin. I pretended to be absorbed in the job and I didn't look up. He was standing close to me and his hand touched my shoulder. "Get your overcoat on – it's going to be cold out there." This time the tears would have been of joy, but again the voice inside me, "Steady, steady. Let that be a lesson to you. Don't take 'em or anything for granted and most important, don't ever show you are hurt."

I grabbed my overcoat, scarf and gloves and turned to rush outside. "Just a minute. Drink some of this tea. We shall be away for a long time." I smiled my thanks, and once again realised that I had the best dad it was possible to have; that also I never forgot.

Outside it seemed to have gone colder and the wind was cutting like a knife. On the far towing path stood a horse, its breath like a cloud of steam. The Ice Boat was already out of its

62

berth and the long towing line was attached to the end facing the way we intended to go. We two latecomers dropped lightly into the well of the boat, the gear was checked, lines right, spare ropes stowed, barge pole in its rack, all present and correct. A shrill whistle from mi dad and the horse under the skilful handling of the boater took the strain and the Ice Boat and its crew moved quickly on their way, followed at once by several pairs of loaded boats, taking full advantage of the cleared passageway ahead.

The colliery and its surroundings were quickly left astern and in less than a couple of minutes we had passed under the Chain Bridge and shot through to Ladyshore Bridge. The lightness of the Ice Boat, compared with the laden weight of the following pairs, enabled the horse to make good walking speed as the ice on this trip was but a skim. The pace did not falter, nor did it vary.

I was at once instructed on the handling of the boat. There was no rudder and direction was controlled by transferring the weight of the crew from one side to the other; the person at the head of the boat gave the lead, followed by the rest of the boat's company. No orders were given and none were necessary – it was a simple procedure and working the boat kept us all warm.

After Ladyshore Bridge I was in strange land with open fields on the far side and the deep valley of the Irwell on the towing path side. Round each turn was something new, and everything was pointed out to me in "running commentary" fashion: "Over there used to be the Stopes Colliery boatbuilding yard, and there was the loading bay for their boats, at the end of a tramway which ran across those fields from the pithead, which was almost a mile from the canal side. There up ahead is Mount Sion Bleachworks; that thing on the banking is their steam crane which they use to lift the loaded boxes out of the boats. Manchester Collieries." (This was said with a touch of disgust.) "That milestone says how many miles to Manchester. Look over there in the reeds – can you see 'em? Water hens. By gum, watch yon rabbit go!" Sometimes we saw a fox. "Aye, Owd Reddihough uz bin afther 'im fer some time," chirped Tommy. "Ee 'as that. Must bi u yar er two nay," another chap put in.

Due to the brisk walking pace of the horse we very soon left the following, heavily-laden boats behind and the plod of the horse's hooves and the swish of our passage through the ice sounded very loud in the quiet of countryside. The cold air was sharp and biting to the face, but I was busy taking instruction, asking and being told what happened in a heavy frost and thick ice. My feet were warm moving from side to side in the boat and perhaps because it was my first trip the crew rolled the "Breaker" with more than the usual vigour, no doubt to "See if wi con get little bugger sick." But apart from one fleeting moment of queasiness I was too absorbed in what was happening to be affected.

63

Ladyshore Colliery (AW)

Suddenly the canal was clear of ice and it looked as though steam was rising off the water. Rounding the turn we saw Waterside Mills, just before Radcliffe; two cotton mills, noisy even on the outside, with fireholes open on to the canal. The surplus steam from the massive engines which drove the mill's machinery discharged into the canal, which was also the source of their water supply. Two men were manually unloading an open coal boat (one which was not fitted with container boxes) directly into the firehole and the firebeater stood, resplendent in a new boiler suit, superintending their work. "Mornin', Rafe," and the reply of "Mornin', Peter," were typical of the many friendly greetings exchanged on the journey. Rounding a shallow turn it was as though we were going along a back street of a row of terraced houses. The gates of the back yards opened directly on to the towing path. We were near to Radcliffe now and there, on the far side, was a workshop. It was not a big one but every time I passed it I never failed to be fascinated: a cooperage. ("A cooperage? Con't not say weer them barrels is made?") It was always a busy place – a family firm employing about half a dozen people, craftsmen and apprentices. This morning, as we drew nearer, a man with a bowler hat perched on the back of his head, his thumbs in his waistcoat armholes, wearing a leather apron with a pipe stuck in the side of his

Radcliffe Wharf, Water Lane, in the 1920's   *(F Sunderland)*

65

mouth, strolled down to the water's edge and called across: "Aw reet, Rafe? Thi fayther aw reet?" Without waiting for a reply he turned on his heel and strolled back to his men. "Who's that?" I said. "That's er... that's er... I don't know his name but I've known him a long time," was the reply I got, and strangely that was the way I continued, on speaking terms, but never able to put a name to him. As the cooper's yard ("Barrel works, yer clever sod") passed by the horse entered a bridge hole and, once through, the canal widened into a large basin and somebody said, "Radcliffe Wharf".

On the far side was the wharf with unloading and storage facilities, a steam crane was puffing away lifting a box of coal out of one of our boats and several more waited to be unloaded. Off to one end a number of empty boats awaited collection. This was Ladyshore's local coal depot.

Greetings were exchanged with the men who were working the boats and with the Agent who appeared at the office doorway. "That's Harry Stott; nice bloke," I was told. For a moment or two the Ice Boat crashed around the basin, breaking up the ice, and then we resumed our journey towards Bury. After leaving Radcliffe we entered the Straight Length. In winter it was perhaps the bleakest part of the canal; there was a vast stretch of open farmland on the far side, the north-east wind came straight off the Pennines and it certainly was cold. In this length the ice was much thicker and the horse had to be put to a trot. The boat was rolled from side to side, the crash of breaking ice filled the air and after less than a hundred yards of this faster pace a shrill whistle brought the horse to a halt. "Have a breather, Duck," and then to me: "Don't put too much strain on our horses; remember that, now." The man on the banking (Owd Duck) was now pulling the boat back a few yards. "That's to give us a clear run into the ice when we start," continued my mentor. A minute or so later he gave another whistle, the slack in the line was taken up, the horse set off at a walking pace and then broke into a trot. The following boat rocked crazily from side to side, or so it seemed; the purpose was to create a wave which would surge ahead and crack the ice so that the boat could smash the floes into fragments.

On we went up this long, straight length; run-halt, run-halt; it was bitterly cold but the physical effort kept me warm, or was it the enthusiasm and sheer joy of working the Ice Boat? "There you are - t'Farmers Arms," and on the far side, in a garden setting, stood a large old public house, and this amid a vast expanse of fields. On the towing path side we had for some distance been running parallel to the railway line, the electric line from Bury to Manchester.

At the far end of the Straight Length we passed under a low bridge and swung away round a left hand turn where on the towing path side we passed a number of terraced cottages, the

66

front doors of which opened on to the canal banking. In the near distance were a number of large buildings, one of which was Crompton's Mill, and a little further on were the warehouses and other buildings of the once-bustling Bury Wharf. Once again, as we came close to the mills, the ice thinned and then cleared altogether.

Again the whistle and the horse stopped; the boat came into the banking. "That's it. Anybody stretching their legs?" I hopped smartly ashore, but not to stretch my legs - I was looking for a convenient wall, and so it seemed was everybody in the crew.

Whilst we were temporarily absent my father had scrambled on to the now tilted deck, unhooked the line from the for'd ringbolt and taken the line aft. Both ends of the boat were alike, so now for'd became aft and aft became for'd.

"It's clear now up to Bury, so let's get back." The tone was now relaxed, Dad had lit a Gold Flake and Owd Duck had his pipe going like a factory chimney. (He was reputed to smoke a mixture related to horses and camels - the pong certainly suggested that.) The others of the crew indulged in their particular vice; cigarettes, pipe or chewing bacca. The cold had a keener bite, perhaps because the boat did not have to be worked in the same way on the return trip as it had on the outward run and it was suggested that I should walk with Owd Duck: "It'll be warmer fo' you."

Owd Duck was a person of reputed wisdom; to me he was a bit of a strange character. He had never been known to indulge in a smile, let alone a laugh, and I thought that to walk with him would give me the chance to get to know him better. The boat came to the side and I stepped on to the towing path and was quickly walking alongside the boater. I was glad that the wind dispersed the aroma of that pipe.

For some distance we plodded along in silence and he did not appear to notice me. In the end I ventured, rather hesitantly, "Do you like being a boater, Mister Duck?" (I was not aware that his name was Haydock as I had never heard him so addressed.) There was no reply and we continued our brisk walking pace. Not to be put off, I

Canal boat horse's harness
(Drawing by Brian Worthington)

asked again: "Mister Duck, have you ever wanted to be anything other than a boater?" Again silence. After a few more yards of walking the pipe was taken from his mouth, a well directed spit or two and then he said, "When thes walkt ut back uv n'orse un smelled un 'orse's fart thi nar wants bi nowt else but uh boather," and with these words of profound wisdom he replaced his pipe and our journey continued in silence, save for the creak of harness and the plod of the horse's feet.

So it was that we came in sight of Radcliffe Wharf, the surface of the path changed to paving stones, the iron-shod hooves rang and the silence of the countryside gave way to town noises. Duck, who had been walking at the horse's rear, his hand on the noose which hooked on to the swindle tree, suddenly said, "Nay, lad, tak owd o'this 'ere un poo 'is arse frum t'cut as ee gus through yon bridge'ole." I was thrilled and delighted at such a display of confidence and I eagerly took hold of the line as directed, proudly stepping out behind the horse. A little lad behind a big horse - and he was a big un! Going through the bridge I did exactly as I had been told, Duck nodded approvingly, and once through my attention wandered and I gazed across the water to the cooper's yard. I did not get the early warning. I failed to see the horse's tail rise stiffly. All I knew was a flush of hot smelly gas in my face and the thudding splash of a hot sticky something on my hand and arm. Duck walked on beside me unconcerned. I let go of the line and shook my arm to get rid of the stuff. It stuck. I removed it with my left hand; I searched the side of the path for some winter grass to clean it off with. There was none, nor was there any old paper about. I looked to wash it off in the canal but the water level was too far below the coping, I searched my pockets for a handkerchief, managing to spread the stuff more over my clothing. Roars of laughter came from the following Ice Boat - it was evident that my antics and frustrated efforts were a source of amusement to the crew. Realising that, I resumed my station in a dignified manner but very warily.

For some time Duck gave no indication that he had noticed anything untoward had happened and then he broke the silence, becoming, for him, talkative: "Allus does it theer on t'road wom. Thes larnt uh lot today, moor as the'l larn i'a lung while. Thes bin crissent, aw reet. Nor awl t'lads is crissent. They'll awlus bi lucky, un t'cut ul awlus bi wi' thi. Un agen, it's 'elthy." There was certainly no answer to the last part of his remarks.

We made good time back to base, even if I did have the healthy odour of a midden, a point of which I was reminded as soon as I entered the warm cabin and stood in front of the fire drinking tea. My parent instructed me to "Take that bucket and get some hot water and get a wash." This I did, sponging my coat as best I could. Of course, a small matter of the smell of horse did not interfere with my eating; I put away ten slices from a large loaf made into sandwiches, as well as two slabs of cake, and still had an empty spot in my stomach. I was offered and accepted part of my dad's dinner; Owd Duck was quite right, "It were 'ealthy." To cap it all, later that afternoon, I was given 4d. "That's Ice Boat money." "Oh, thanks very much." To a lad on two shillings a week spending money, that was very acceptable. All in all it had been a good day, a splendid day, and I was again looking forward and hoping.

Nothing was said when I called at my grandparents' house on my way home (this we did every evening), but no sooner had I crossed our own doorstep than my mother came into the kitchen, sniffed and then said: "Horse. Wherever have you been? Get that coat off, and your boots, go and have a bath. There is some Lifebuoy soap in the bathroom; use plenty of it. Go on now, you stink!" After my ablutions, clean and once again acceptable, I sat and really enjoyed my tea.

My coat sleeve, in fact my whole coat, had been scrubbed, my boots I had washed and cleaned, and wearing a fresh pair of trousers the following morning I smelled, so I thought, rather pleasant. Or I did think so until I arrived at work. The first person I met was Little Tommy, my friend and self-appointed protector. He wrinkled his nose and then asked, "Wot's that stink?" "What stink?" I asked, taken aback. "It's thi jacket agen; weer'st bin?" "Oh, that's some scent of mi mother's, Old English Lavender." "It met be; it bloody stinks worse ner 'orse muck," and on that friendly note we started the working day.

During that winter the Ice Boat was out with regularity under varying conditions and on each trip my course of instruction was continued – from skims to very thick ice. Some of the operations involved the use of a team of three horses and my father made sure that I was able to handle the craft and the team with competence. By the end of that winter I was told that I had made very good progress and that by the next winter it was possible that I could take charge. (I had already made one or two trips in command but under supervision.)

Throughout the summer months I was, by example, instruction and lecture, trained how to treat and handle men and this fitted very well with the activities I had undertaken outside of work. The next winter, after the first trip of the frost, I was told, "Next time you are on your own." The original build-up of anticipatory excitement was now a thing of the past, but I must own to looking forward to the next freeze and a week later there started a long spell of Arctic weather – heavy frost and thick, freezing fog.

Keeping open a navigable passage was the responsibility of the Canal Company and for that purpose they had their own Ice Boat, the *Sarah Lansdale*. It was a large, well-founded craft, but one such ice-breaker could not service all the lengths at a time convenient to the colliery companies who used the canal.

In the early days the coal owners who operated large fleets built their own Ice Boats and undertook the responsibility of keeping open the lengths most vital to their own trade, so ensuring the efficient working of the canal in winter. This was a very acceptable arrangement which worked to the advantage of all concerned for many years. However, collieries had closed or they had been absorbed into larger groups in which canal transport did not play a vital part and by the time that I became a very small cog in the local canal system, Ladyshore Coal Company (1930) Ltd was the major user of the top lengths, Bolton to Bury. Manchester Collieries sent an average of two pairs of boats a week to Mount Sion Bleach Works at Stopes and the understanding then was that the lengths from Farnworth Bridge (E P Potter & Company, Chemical Works) to Bury Wharf were the responsibility of Ladyshore, whilst the locks at Nob End and the entire lower lengths into Oldfield Road, Salford, were taken care of by the Canal people, who also, in times of keen frost, supplied several of their men to help the crew of the Ladyshore boat when requested.

On the morning that I first took charge of the Ice Boat the people who came from the Company had never been with us before. The ice was thick, even round the colliery area, and as we had only two horses available for towing it meant that greater efforts were required from the crew. The boat had to be rocked with considerable vigour. The Company chaps had only had experience of breaking ice in the *Sarah Lansdale,* which was a very heavy boat steered by a rudder, its breaking effectiveness being the sheer weight of the boat and its crew and they had not been called upon to swing the boat about.

At the beginning of the trip that day I did not expect any complications, but it soon became evident that working the boat our way and as the circumstances demanded was not the intention of the Company contingent. They also made it very clear that they did not take kindly to a youngster having command. This resulted in the greater part of the heavy work, and it was heavy work, falling on Tommy, another of our men, and myself. Consequently the "runs" were shorter and we were taking more out of our horses. This bothered me, and it also made the boaters rather resentful. My father would not have had the least trouble; he would have given orders once and if they had not been promptly carried out the culprits would have been blasted. He never used swear words; as a pillar of the Church, his view was that that was wrong, but there was never any misunderstanding as to the meaning of his verbal lashings.

But on that day I mistakenly thought that such a course of action would have been wrong, so at the start the three of us pulled our guts out. Also, I have never been able to whistle; try as I might the resulting sound was pathetic. So for signalling I used a whistle which I wore on a lanyard round my neck. Our own people did not see anything in this but necessity; the Company men saw it as swank. It was in such an atmosphere of non-co-operation that we slogged our way to Radcliffe, with runs of twenty to thirty yards at a time, keeping only a short distance ahead of the following loaded boats.

When we got to Radcliffe we had to thrash about in the Depot area more than usual and by some mischance one of the lines snagged. The frozen rope seemed to be part of the deck structure – it was solid – and efforts to free it by lashing the line about were to no avail. The boat hook was ineffective when applied from the banking, the foredeck and the ring bolts were a mass of ice, and Duck, who was on the towing path, so rightly remarked, "Thel do no good wi' that."

Canal at Scotson Fold

(F Sunderland)

Maybe it was my short temper, certainly a lack of discretion, and it was by no means bravery that prompted me to scramble on to the icy deck on hands and knees. I took hold of the frozen rope in my gloved hand and by pushing and tugging I at last got a movement. It was almost loose when suddenly the deck tilted crazily and my hand was caught in a vice-like grip. "Hell! I've broken my hand!" My body slipped crosswise on the narrow deck, feet over the water, and my hand was slipping out of my glove. In seconds I would be off that deck and into the freezing water, then thud! in the middle of my back and I was being pulled. In the distance (or so it sounded) a voice said, "Get ******* boat level!" and I felt the cant ease. Hands took hold of my ankles and together with the pull on my coat I was drawn back into the well of the boat and helped to a seat on the step.

I was cold, bloody cold inside; it was the first time that I experienced not the fire, but the iciness of my temper. I was appalled that grown men would try to "take the shit out of the little sod" in such a dangerous manner (I had a lot to learn, now I know). Anyway, the pantomime stopped there and then and I heard Tommy's voice from a long way off, "Art aw reet, lad?" "Yes, I am that," I replied, then, "Thanks, and thanks to you, Duck." I did not know the right course to take but I think I did what was expected. Turning to the Company men I said something like: "I've had a bloody bellyful! Either you do the job without any more buggering about or on to the banking you go and make your way back. Otherwise we will proceed on our journey." After a pause I spoke to Duck, who was grinning from ear to ear: "Right, pal, let's go." As the horses were taking the strain, Tommy replaced the boat hook in the rack and muttered, "Un bloody time too."

We had no further trouble and went up the Straight Length, tough as it was, running, halting, as laid down in the manual of instruction, with the boat rolling in the approved manner. The Company men worked as well and enthusiastically as our own people. We had to go right up into Bury Wharf and clear the ice there as well, the frost having been so keen.

The boaters had brought along brew cans (well, the horses had carried them) and without any prompting one of our men had taken them into Crompton's firehole to get hot water. With Tommy's help I got the boat ready for the return trip. The crew stood on the banking drinking tea and then looking for places of convenience. One of the Company men called across, "Come on, some tay fer thi," to which I replied, "Thanks" and went along to join the group. The can lid had already been passed to several people; it had last been washed about the time of the Armistice in 1918, but even so the hot tea tasted really good and was welcome. The chap who had called me over put his hand on my arm. "Sorry abayt back yon," he apologised. "What? Oh, that. I should have known better; it was a good job

Duck was about," to which reply he gave a nod of approval.

The loaded boats which had followed us up to Bury had been safely delivered, empties had been collected and now the convoy was ready for the return journey. So it was with a "Right, chaps," that we again climbed aboard and moved off smartly, destination Little Lever.

The frost was so keen that we had to break up the ice again down the Straight Length, even though it was less than an hour since the loaded boats had gone through on the run to Bury. Nevertheless we maintained a good walking pace and the following little fleet was not hard put to it to keep close to our stern. Everybody worked well and pleasantly and very soon we were at Radcliffe. This time it was possible to exchange the usual pleasantries and greetings. The question, "Weer is ee?" was answered with "He's not out today." "Tell 'im wi were axin." "I will." There was an attempt by Tommy to give a song, but he was discouraged with references to adverse weather conditions. By and large the journey home was rather robust and it was a boatload of hungry men (and a lad) who tied up at Ladyshore about 2.00pm.

Our return to base was watched with what we took to be some anxiety by mi dad. He found no fault because there were no shouted instructions; the boaters and the horses had gone to the stables, the crew had landed and made for the warmth of the cabin and Tommy and myself attended to the mooring of the boat and collecting the gear. As we were watched from a distance, and my father being slightly deaf (when he did not want to hear) I took the chance of saying to Tommy: "Think on. Not a word to him, not a bloody single word or he won't let me go again." He stopped in his task, looked me in the eye and said rather indignantly, "Wot's up wi' thee? There's nowt fer t'tell 'im, is there? Ah dern't know. wot thet on abayt." It was with a feeling of relief that I muttered my thanks. As we walked to the dock I tried to whistle, resulting in a dirty look from my mate and a, "Wilt give ower? Tha makes mi grind mi teeth." How could I? He did not have a tooth in his head.

As we deposited the gear I told him to go and get his dinner and I went up to the Colliery Offices. "Please may I have the Ice Boat money?" I asked, and then told them how many people had been involved. For each person I was given 4d and back in the cabin I handed out this wealth and then sat contentedly engaged in my favourite pastime, eating.

It was then mi dad asked, "Everything go all right for you today? No problems?" and through a mouthful of potato pie, "No." Again, after a pause, "None?" and again, "No." What was up with him? There the conversation rested; if ever he got to know, it was never mentioned.

For several years up to the outbreak of war I took charge of the Ice Boat, and often the same people came from the Company to augment our crew. Our relationship was always good; the Ice Boat was my command, mine by right.

ICE BOAT MONEY

At the time of the building of the Manchester, Bolton and Bury Canal payment for work done was often supplemented with ale and in the lists of accounts for that time statements will be found such as:

To sawing. Jose. Thomas and mate, Three shillings and Ale

It is stated in the Company minutes that Nightingale, nephew of Matthew Fletcher, objected to the extra ale, but it was such established practice in canal circles that his objection was ignored.

When the waterway became operational the 4d per day was given as an extra bonus to the ice breaker crews with the intention that they should enjoy a pint of hot mulled ale. In later years this practice was discontinued by everyone with the exception of the Fletcher family at Ladyshore, and whilst the original 4d was never increased, its payment was continued as long as their boats used the canal.

Bolton Wharf   *(Bolton Library)*

Learning to Swim

The canal, just like any other deep water, must always have been an attraction to those hardy souls who revelled in this element and even though (in the 1930's) swimming baths had for a long time been open to the public both in Farnworth and Bolton, summer weekends saw large numbers of young people congregating at Nob End. The locks were used as an open air swimming pool or lido; could it have been that mixed bathing was not allowed at that time in the public baths? Of course, there were no changing facilities; there was certainly no privacy and many of the intending swimmers went along wearing swimming costumes under their clothing. But there were always those who either did not have swimwear or had forgotten to bring it along. Such a trivial matter was not allowed to interfere with their pleasure – neither the lads' nor the lasses' – and it was a case of starkers and no blushes.

Many people who worked on the canal were unable to swim, even though the opportunity and in some cases the necessity was ever present, sometimes with near fatal results. Often I was asked, "As arr farn in?" and for some time after I first started work on the waterway I could honestly say "No."

I do not say that I was afraid of falling in; I was certainly not afraid of water and I had for some time been going to the baths attempting to learn to swim, without much success. But the canal was a different thing altogether. In places the stone banking rose at least two and a half feet above water level and this made me wary of falling in. However, familiarity breeds contempt, and this is the story of how I eventually learned to swim.

I was at the time about sixteen years of age. In addition to the boat dock, my father was responsible for the maintenance of all surface plant as well as overseeing the general maintenance of the pit shafts and winding gear, not only at Ladyshore but at the pumping station at Farnworth Bridge. This place was very important in controlling the water problems in the Ladyshore workings and periodically we had to spend some time maintaining the plant and equipment at "top pit", as it was called.

Our entire gang had been there for several days and work was being carried out on one of the big air compressors which provided the motive power for most of the machinery down the pit at Ladyshore. Drilling machines, pumps and winches were worked by compressed air. By mistake certain essential tools had not been packed and were needed at once, so I was summoned. "Here is a list of what we need. Get on your bike

and fetch them, and don't let it take you so long," were the
instructions I was given in a no-nonsense voice which I knew
well enough. It was a nice morning and I didn't like top pit
anyway, so I was glad of the chance to get a change for a bit.
I was on my way at once, rode down the blue wall length and
made the right hand turn across from Top o't'Lodge, where
there is a splendid view down the Croal Valley (though it was
lost on me). I pedalled into the approaches of the Company
Depot, along past the stonemasons' yard and round the next
turn to the depot proper. Here I stopped, leaned the bike
against the wall and went to the blacksmith's shop, where I
leaned on the bottom half of the stable-type door and watched
the smith at work on red hot iron. It was something I had seen
hundreds of times and yet it was always interesting, and after
a minute or so the smith looked up. "It's thee, is it?" (This
was the greeting I always got.) "Ast nowt do? If thes not, ah
'ave, un if yon Lunn sees thee stonnin' theer, ee'l reckon ahv
not nayther," and then he added, "Bi gooin'm wilt?" My friends
had rather funny ways of expressing pleasure on seeing me; as
for being welcome, I sometimes wondered.

Leaving the Company Depot I crossed the top of the locks by the
little wooden bridge, then rode down the slope to the towing
path again and pedalled along to Bailey Bridge. (It was on

Hall Lane Bridge   *(Bolton Evening News)*

this length that in a few years' time the banking, perched as it was over the River Irwell, would collapse so disastrously as to speed the end of the Manchester, Bolton and Bury Canal.) Through the bridge I went at speed; it was a good job there was nobody coming in my direction, and in a flash I was down the dip and over the waggon road used by Broadbent's paper mill, which stood far below on the river bank. Rounding the next turn, there was a view of the Irwell at the bottom of the valley. It was comforting to think that the towing path was well fenced on that side and one got the feeling, "It's a long drop down there, mate."

Ladyshore was now in sight and soon I was carrying my bike up the steps of the chain bridge which crossed over the canal and led on to the pit brow. It was then that I saw one of the chaps from the office coming over the yard. I went past the blacksmith's shop, down another flight of steps and made my way to the boat dock. It was only a matter of minutes to collect the tools which had been listed; there was no tea and it was too much trouble to make any. Furthermore my instructions had been: "Don't let it take you so long." Setting off back, I wondered why go to the trouble of two lots of steps, carrying my bike and the extra weight, then over the brow and bridge? By taking the far side I could be at Bailey Bridge in the time that would take. Good thinking, lad.

Admittedly I had only once walked this section, but I did not remember any snags and as I had so often seen it from the towing path and it had looked all right – a good stone coping and then a grass verge before the boundary fence – off I went. At first it was easy riding on the wide coping, along the lengths of loaded boats tied two abreast, on down t'clough and along the edge of the turning hole. The cut looked a hell of a width here and I'd been told it was very deep too. Going round on to a straight, there up in front was Bailey Bridge and not far to go. Suddenly the space between the fence and the coping narrowed and the coping was covered with slimy moss where the water draining from the high land on the other side of the fence ran into the cut. Whoops! Splash! Me and my bike went in and I couldn't swim. I was fully clothed, with heavy boots, the banking was a long way off and there was nobody about, nor likely to be. Panic! I attempted a stroke or two; the banking was nearer but a long way up. Another struggle and my feet hit something – a foothold. My fingers found a crevice in the stonework and then another; the foothold was taking the weight and I was able to reach the far side of the coping. There was a deep ridge where the draining water had formed a pool and with both hands I heaved, and again. "Oh Lord, please don't let me slip back!" With another heave my chest was on the coping, my hand grasped a stout fence post and like a cork out of a bottle I was on the banking, shivering and scared stiff. I rolled over to the fence, wrapped my arms round

77

the woodwork and lay there sobbing for breath for what seemed to be a long time. Then I carefully got to my feet and climbed through the fence. What was I to do now? "Get home as quick as you can, lad, and get some dry clothes." So off I set, squelching over the rough grass with the fence between me and the now unfriendly canal. The bike? I never gave it or the tools a thought. I got to the bridge and made my way up the short. hill to the roadway which went to Nob End; by now most of the water had squelched out of the laceholes of my boots but my soggy clothes, particularly my trousers, were very uncomfortable. It was hard work and there was no point in stopping at the Company Depot so I hurried on down the hill to the basin, over the wooden footbridge and on to the Vat Waste towards Wilson's Bridge over the Croal and then up the very steep Wilson's Brow to Cemetery Road. My grandparents lived just at the top of the Brow and if I had called there I should have had a lot of explaining to do, so on I went, my drying clothes a leaden weight and the running and walking, running and walking sapping my energy. I climbed the incline of Peel Street with the thought that my bedraggled appearance would most certainly attract attention. My family were well known locally and I dreaded meeting anyone who knew me. The road home now was more on the level but led through the main streets of Farnworth and my running and walking was from preference along the back streets. At last I arrived at our front gate and made my way along the garden path to the back door. I had hoped that my mother would be out shopping, but no, there she was in the kitchen. "Whatever have you been up to again? You're soaked. I hope you've not got another cold," and then her favourite phrase, "You stink, too; get your clothes off here and go and get a bath."

Soon I was bathed and dressed in clean dry clothes, smelling of Lifebuoy soap. I went downstairs and was called upon for a blow by blow account of my experience, which was given whilst I sat and had some dinner. Part way through this I suddenly realised that it was Friday – payday. I stopped eating and I must have gone white. "Now what is the matter? Are you ill?" I felt the colour returning to my cheeks. "It's Friday," I replied. "Well?" I looked with surprise and then added, "I haven't got my wage. I shall have to go back." Reluctantly I left the table, got my hat and coat and was quickly on my way. There was no need now to run but I made good time (no need to keep off the main roads either) down into Farnworth, over Market Street and down Peel Street, on past Farnworth Station and into Cemetery Road. I wasn't calling at Grandad's, not likely, not till I was going home. One lot of explaining would be more than enough. Grandma wouldn't be content with once telling and she had a very sharp, biting tongue, so on I went.

The remainder of the journey did not take long. I was soon

passing through Bailey Bridge and round the next turn, and then I saw a group of men on the far banking. As I drew nearer I could see they were: Mr Hayward, the Colliery Manager, Jim Edge, the chap who worked in the office, little Tommy, several other people and my father. They had boat hooks and grappling irons which they were dragging about in the canal. To one side against the railings was my bike. I stopped and watched and after a bit I called across to them, "What's up?" and Jim Edge answered, without looking to see who the questioner was, "It's Little Rafe's lad – he's gone in here." (Never in all the time I worked on the canal did I have a name of my own, I was always "Little Rafe's lad".) "Oh aye," I said, and then one or the other looked up. They saw me standing there, and for a moment I was thankful that there was water between us! I rather think they were sorry that I was not deep down; well, their remarks gave me that impression. The conversation, as we made our way to Ladyshore, me on one side and them on the other, was very one-sided. Trundling along their equipment and my bike did not interfere with their ability to keep up a fluent chorus of invective. Needless to say, I kept my distance when we arrived at the Boat Dock and I was also very thankful that I was at night school that evening; it saved a lot of earache.

This incident took longer than any other to live down, and the fact that I was afterwards able to swim (a little) was not even taken into consideration. Some weeks later I said as much to Tommy (when we were again on speaking terms) and got answered with, "Ee were upset when ee thowt they'd draynt." "What? He clouted me round me ear'ole." "Aye, bur nobbot won ee thinks a lot abayt thee, dus Little Rafe. It were 'is road uh showin' ee were glad fer t'see thi," and once again, as so often with Tommy, there was no answer to that.

The remarkable scene where the canal burst its banks, leaving a coal barge half suspended over the chasm.

CATARACT OF WATER FROM BOLTON—BURY CANAL

THOUSANDS OF TONS OF EARTH IN RIVER

of the men who lives near to the office. The water was pouring down and throwing dirt and rock very nearly as high as the canal bank."

Barge Disappears

Another early witness of the burst was Mrs. John Holden, whose home, 20, Boscow-rd., overlooks the canal. "My husband, a mule spinner at the Irwell Bank mill," she told the "Evening News" "rises about 6 o'clock in

The Final Years

By the time that I had reached my seventeenth birthday I was aware that the future of the Canal was short. Traffic, with the exception of Ladyshore coal, had ceased on the top lengths and although my father was reluctant to admit it, the prospects were not rosy. It was then that I turned my thoughts to an entirely different career away from the canal altogether. I realised, of course, that I had a further four years to do before I was "out of my time" and even though I was prepared to see this through, many arguments and heated discussions took place at home. My courses of study at night school were stepped up and I became politically minded and interested in public speaking, with my mother's certain approval. Every penny I could scrape was put away with the idea of starting up in business; finishing my apprenticeship was now a chore.

The summer of 1936 brought the final disaster to the Canal. Early one morning the length from the top of the locks to Bailey Bridge breached and through this roared thousands of gallons of water, depositing many tons of rock and rubble into the valley of the Irwell far below. The scene was one of desolation; boats were torn from their moorings and at least one was smashed to pieces in the river bed and another was left teetering on the edge of the crevasse. This was disaster of the first magnitude and there could now be no doubt that the Manchester, Bolton and Bury Canal was doomed. The Company certainly had no intention of spending the vast sum of money which would be needed to effect the repair – the traffic did not warrant it – and yet it was almost twenty years later that the lengths from Ladyshore to Bury closed to traffic.

The once-busy waterway was now in a pathetic state and more than ever I wanted to get away. I thought perhaps I should, but jobs were hard to get in the 1930's so I stayed on until the outbreak of war.

Recently I paid one of my now very rare visits to Manchester, and whilst the bustle of the city is always a tonic, I wondered how many of those smartly dressed men of business appreciate the importance of the humble and often despised "cut" to Manchester's commercial success. Do the crowds in Bolton's superior shopping centre realise how much they owe to the now non-existent canal? Do the people of Bury ever think of what the canal did for them? If the Manchester, Bolton and Bury Canal had not been built by those far-sighted businessmen of the 1790's, and worked with so much enthusiasm for so many years by the canal people, the vast industrial area represented by these three centres would not have figured so prominently in the industrial history of our country.

Coal is too costly

LADYSHORE PIT TO BE CLOSED DOWN

The last of the Ladyshore pit ponies

One of last pits in country to use naked candles

One of the last coal mines in Great Britain to retain candle illumination and the last in Lancashire to use ponies, Ladyshore Pit, Little Lever, which has been worked for more than a hundred years, is to be closed down this weekend. The 260 workers there received their notices a week ago and have been offered jobs at other pits in the Leigh and Tyldesley areas.

"Sentence of death" was passed on the pit in July last year when it was stated that costs of operation were too high. The production of 1,250 tons of coal per week was costing 12s. a ton more than its selling price.

A reprieve was granted when it was stated there could be an improvement in output and plans were announced for the provision of a full-meal canteen. After a start had been made, however, the project was abandoned, probably because the improvement in production had been only slight and irregular.

A Coal Board official told the "Journal" this week that the Board have been negotiating for ... viously been amalgamated unde ... "Lancashire Associated Col ...

Farnworth Journal, June 3rd 1949   *(Farnworth Library)*

****

For a current list of local history publications available by post, please send a stamped addressed envelope to Neil Richardson, 88 Ringley Road, Stoneclough, Radcliffe, Manchester M26 9ET.

****